ORKN

FOLK
TALES

ORKNEY
FOLK TALES

TOM MUIR

ILLUSTRATED BY
SHEILA FAICHNEY

The
History
Press

Dedicated to my dear friend and fellow storyteller,
Lawrence Tulloch of Shetland. We have shared many
adventures around the world and I am proud to call him
my brother; if not by blood then by choice.

© Sheila Faichney, illustrations
© Tom O'Brien, author photograph

First published 2014

The History Press
The Mill, Brimscombe Port
Stroud, Gloucestershire, GL5 2QG
www.thehistorypress.co.uk

Reprinted in 2016

British Library Cataloguing in Publication Data.
A catalogue record for this book is available from the British Library.

ISBN 978 0 7524 9905 5

Typesetting and origination by The History Press
Printed in Great Britain

CONTENTS

INTRODUCTION

The Orkney Islands lie just north of the furthest-most tip of Scotland, separated by the Pentland Firth where the waters of the Atlantic Ocean and the North Sea converge in a violent struggle. Orkney, as it is simply known, is made up of around seventy islands, some large and some small, and has a population of around 20,000. The smaller islands are called 'holms' (a term still used in Scandinavia), where sheep are sometimes taken to graze. It has been said that the definition of a holm is an island with enough grass on it to fatten one sheep, feed two or starve three. This is a slight exaggeration, but only just. The islands are generally low-lying, flat and fertile. Farming has been the main stay of living for thousands of years as the rich, fertile soil is good for growing grass and cereal crops.

The first Orcadians (as the people of Orkney are known) were here during the Mesolithic period and the remains of flint tools used by those nomadic hunter-gatherers are found in small numbers around the islands. One site has been carbon dated to 8,000 years ago. During the Neolithic, Orkney supported a large population that built in stone, as trees on the islands were not as large and plentiful as they were in Scotland. Buildings are therefore preserved, including the Knap of Howar in Papa Westray; at 5,500 years old, these are the oldest standing stone buildings in Northern Europe.

The 5,000-year-old village of Skara Brae contains furniture made of stone, while the dead were taken to their final resting place in the numerous tombs that cover the islands; the houses of the dead. The finest example of which, Maeshowe, is built so that the midwinter sun shines its setting rays up the long entrance passage and illuminates the chamber within. Standing stones and stone circles mark another way of thinking about the world in which the Neolithic people lived and they have remained special places for generations of Orcadians. A huge Neolithic temple complex is being excavated at the time of writing at the Ness of Brodgar, and now it seems that the great ceremonial stone circles originated here in the north and spread south.

The 'brochs', huge circular stone towers from the Iron Age, around 2,000 years ago, are scattered throughout the islands, suggesting a time of conflict and violence. The Picts, late Iron Age people, carved their enigmatic symbol stones in Orkney, as well as in their heartland in the Highlands. What the fate of the Picts was we simply do not know, but the Vikings from Norway arrived at the end of the eighth century and took possession of the islands. Pictish culture disappeared from the archaeological record, replaced by Viking traditions as the Norwegian settlers came west over the sea to farm the fertile land and to fish in the sea that encircles the islands. The Vikings also gave the islands their current names and the Norn language, a dialect of Old Norse, was still spoken in parts of Orkney until the early nineteenth century. The Earldom of Orkney in the mid-eleventh century, under Earl Thorfinn the Mighty, was said to include Shetland, all the north of Scotland, the Western Isles and part of Ireland. At the beginning of the twelfth century, in 1137, the beautiful red sandstone cathedral of St Magnus was founded, dedicated to a martyred earl who was killed during a time of civil war. This century was seen as the Golden Age of Orkney and its story is told in the *Orkneyinga Saga*, the only Icelandic Saga to be set in Britain.

Orkney was pawned to Scotland by King Christian I of Norway and Denmark in 1468, when he couldn't raise the money to pay the dowry of his daughter Margaret on her marriage to King James III of Scotland. Shetland followed in 1469, but the dowry was never paid, leaving the Northern Isles as part of Scotland. The islands suffered a period of excessive taxation, land grabbing and tyranny under Scottish rule. To this day many islanders consider themselves Orcadian and not Scottish and there are still strong ties to Norway. When Mary Queen of Scots ruled over Scotland she made her half-brother, Robert Stewart, the Earl of Orkney. His cruelty and greed was legendary, but if he was bad then his son Patrick who followed him was worse. 'Black Patie', as he was known, became an Orkney bogeyman used to frighten unruly children into obedience; 'Watch out, or Black Patie will get you!' In 1615 Black Patie was publically beheaded in Edinburgh on a charge of treason having fallen afoul of his paranoid cousin, King James VI of Scotland (James I of England). His reputation was so bad that an old legend has it that his execution had to be delayed in order for him to learn the Lord's Prayer.

Orkney carried on with large landowners, called 'lairds', filling the power vacuum. As the centuries passed these lairds grew, both in their power and their excesses, as is recalled in many stories. Their reign eventually ended after the First World War, when land taxes made these large estates economically unviable. The Crofters Act of 1886 also gave their often abused tenants' rights which their grandparents could never have dreamed of. During  the turbulent twentieth century, Orkney saw the huge natural harbour of Scapa Flow used as a naval base in both world wars. This brought hundreds of thousands of servicemen and women to Orkney; some of whom married and settled here.

So why am I telling you all this? This is supposed to be a book of folk tales, not a history. Well, you must excuse me, but I think that you cannot understand Orkney unless you have at least a brief background of its history. Here, more so than most places, we live alongside our history. Our past and our present exist side by side. Also, the different people who settled here brought with them their own stories and beliefs. The creatures of Orkney's folklore are a mixture of Celtic and Scandinavian, with the emphasis on the latter. In Orkney it is possible to go to a place and see the actual spot where a fiddler played for the trows, or where a mermaid carried off a young man to her city under the sea. The sands where the selkie folk dance are as real as any cathedral, broch or tomb. Orkney is a special place and its stories are its hidden jewels.

But let me introduce myself. My name is Tom Muir and I first saw the light of day at Valdigar in Tankerness at 10.30 p.m. on Thursday, 13 June 1963. Light of day at 10.30 p.m.? Yes; in summer the nights are long and the sun has still not set at that hour. 'Valdigar', which in the Old Norse means the farm of Valdis (the name of the Viking who settled there and broke the soil), is a small farm in the East Mainland parish of Tankerness.

My father, Johnny Muir, was born in the island of Sanday in 1911, while my mother, Lizzie Drever, was born in the island of Westray in 1922. I was a latecomer; the youngest of a family of six and I was a feral child, forever wandering along the shore or in the uncultivated fields where wild flowers grow and wild birds nest. I was very close to nature and had a strong feeling of being a part of Orkney.

I was a school dropout, branded as slow and worthless. Dyslexia was not diagnosed in those days, so I overcame it by myself. I also had a hunger for myths, folk tales and all things old. I am a self-confessed book addict. I gathered all the Orkney stories of supernatural creatures into one book, *The Mermaid Bride; and Other Orkney Folk Tales*, published in 1998, as well as writing many other books.

As a teenager I had left the farm and joined an archaeological dig, which set me on the path to working in the Orkney Museum. I became a storyteller by accident (although, on reflection, I always have been), and many of the stories that I'd like to share with you in this book have connections both to Orkney's history and to my own family. They are written as I would tell them, to give you a taste of an evening of Orkney storytelling, and they contain snippets of family history and information. The stories are brought to life by the illustrations that have been created by my good friend Sheila Faichney. She has breathed life into the stories, for which I thank her. I hope that you will enjoy these tales and maybe, just for a moment, smell the sweet fragrance of the meadow-sweet on the warm summer breeze, hear the song of the lark singing in the skies and catch the gentle lapping of the waves on an Orkney shore.

Tom Muir, 2014

The Orkney Isles

Papa Westray

North Ronaldsay

Westray

Sanday

Eday

Rousay

Stronsay

Egilsay

Wyre

Gairsay

West Mainland

Shapinsay

Kirkwall

Stromness

Graemsay

East Mainland

Hoy

Flotta

Burray

South Ronaldsay

1

EARTH, SEA AND SKY

When the Vikings came to Orkney they brought with them their stories, including this one, which is a great favourite of mine. You can see the origin of it in the myth of the Midgarth Serpent; one of the monstrous offspring of the evil god Loki. This huge sea serpent had grown so large that it was wrapped right around the world and bit its own tail. It would eventually be slain by the god Thor at Ragnorok, the battle at the end of time, but the poison that it spewed over him would also bring about his death.

ASSIPATTLE AND THE STOOR WORM

There was once a farmer who lived in a fine farm called Leegarth, which lay in a valley by the side of a stream. The farmer had a wife and seven sons, and they all worked hard on the farm. Well, that's not strictly true, you see, the parents and six elder sons worked hard, but the youngest son did nothing but lie beside the fire, raking through the ashes, so they called him Assipattle, which means ash raker. Assipattle regularly became covered with ashes and when he went out the ash would blow from him like smoke from a bonfire. The boy was also a great storyteller although in his stories he was always the hero who killed the dragon and married the princess. His brothers hated him and they would kick him on their way out the door, while his parents would just shake their heads sadly when they looked at him.

Now, one day a terrible thing happened; the Stoor Worm arrived at the land where Assipattle lived. This was no ordinary stoor worm, but the Mester Stoor Worm, the oldest, biggest and baddest stoor worm in the sea. A sea monster so big that it was wrapped right around the world, and when it moved it caused earthquakes and tidal waves. It could crush the mightiest ship between the forks of its tongue, or sweep whole villages into its mouth, and if that wasn't bad enough, its breath was poisonous and would kill any living thing it touched. What was worse, it was now lying off the coast of the land where Assipattle lived and it had started to yawn. This was a bad sign because it didn't mean that the Stoor Worm was tired, it meant that it was hungry and it wanted to be fed.

The king gathered together all his advisers and asked them what could be done. No one had any idea, but one of them, who was slightly smarter than the rest, suggested that they ask the Spaeman who lived on the side of the mountain. A spaeman is a wizard, and this one was the cleverest man in all the kingdom. He had a long white beard and carried a staff in his hand. He gave the problem much thought before speaking, saying:

> Your Majesty, the Stoor Worm has travelled all over the world and eaten all sorts of exotic people, but now it is old and has developed a bit of a sweet tooth. If you were to feed it seven maidens for its breakfast every Saturday morning, then it would spare the rest of the kingdom.

So, every Saturday morning seven maidens were bound hand and foot and placed on a flat rock in front of the Stoor Worm's head. When it woke, it yawned seven great yawns and then flicked out its tongue and picked the girls up, one by one, between the forks of its tongue, gobbling them up like sweeties.

One Saturday morning, Assipattle and his family went to see the Stoor Worm eat his terrible breakfast. The old man went white. 'There will soon be no more girls left in this land,' he cried, 'and I have seven sons. Who will they marry? Who will look after us in our old age if there are no more children?'

'Don't worry,' said Assipattle, 'I'll fight the Stoor Worm, and kill it!'

His brothers laughed and threw stones at him until he ran away.

That evening his mother told Assipattle to go to the barn where his brothers were threshing corn and tell them to come in for their supper. Assipattle went to the barn calling, 'Eh, boys; supper's ready.'

'Get him!' shouted his eldest brother, and they all jumped on top of him and covered him with straw.

They would have smothered him if their father hadn't gone out to see what was going on. He wasn't very happy, because it's kind of bad form to try to kill your brother. He gave them a smack on the lug as they went past him and he sent them to the house. He was still scolding them later at the table, but Assipattle said, 'It's all right father, if you hadn't come in when you did I was just about to give them all a damned good thrashing!'

'Well, why didn't you?' sneered his eldest brother.

'Because I'm saving my strength.'

'You? Saving your strength?' Laughed his brother. 'What are you saving your strength for?'

'For when I fight the Stoor Worm, of course!' said Assipattle.

His father shook his head and said, 'You'll fight the Stoor Worm when I make spoons from the horns of the moon!'

Time passed, and more maidens were fed to the Stoor Worm. Soon the people complained that this couldn't be allowed to carry on. The king called the Spaeman back to his palace and asked him what could be done to get rid of the monster for once and for all.

'Well,' said the Spaeman, 'there is one thing that would satisfy the Stoor Worm, but it is too terrible to say.'

'Say it,' shouted the king, 'and that is an order!'

'Well,' said the Spaeman, 'if you were to feed it the most beautiful maiden in the land; your daughter, the Princess Gem de Lovely, then it would go away and spare your kingdom.'

'No!' shouted the court officials. 'That is too high a price to pay.'

But the king raised his hand and said, 'No; it is only right that my daughter, my only child, descended from the god Odin and heir to my kingdom, should die so that her people can live. But, I crave one indulgence. Give me three weeks to find a hero who can fight and kill the Stoor Worm. If anyone can do that I will give him my magic sword, Sikkersnapper, my kingdom and my daughter's hand in marriage.'

A proclamation went throughout the land asking for a hero to fight the Stoor Worm. Thirty-six brave knights rode into town, but when the first dozen saw the size of the Stoor Worm they rode right through the town, out the other side of the town and away home again. The second dozen fainted, and had to be carried out on stretchers, boots first. The third dozen sank into a deep depression and skulked in the king's castle, drinking his beer and wine. The king looked at them and he was disgusted, because the blood of an older and nobler race ran through his veins!

'Bring me my sword, Sikkersnapper,' he ordered, 'and make ready a boat. Tomorrow at dawn I will fight the Stoor Worm, or die in the attempt.'

News of this spread like wildfire throughout the kingdom; the king was going to fight the Stoor Worm. At Leegarth Assipattle was lying by the side of the fire. He was listening to his parents who were lying in their bed, and they were arguing.

'So, the king is going to fight the Stoor Worm,' said Assipattle's father, 'we can take my horse Teetgong; he's the fastest horse in the land, you know.'

'Yeah!' snorted his wife, in a disapproving voice.

'What's up with you tonight?' asked Assipattle's father. 'You're in a very sour mood.'

'And so I might be,' retorted his wife.

'Why? What have I done now?' asked the poor old man.

'You are keeping secrets from me, and I don't like it!'

'Why? What secrets am I keeping? I don't have any secrets from you, my dear.'

'Well, that horse of yours.'

'Teetgong; fastest horse in the land, you know!'

'I know,' she snapped, 'but there's something that you do that makes that horse run so fast, and I want to know what it is.'

'But, my dear, I can't tell you that.'

'And why not?'

'Well – because – you see – it's a – kind of – a – secret.'

'Ah, ha!' said his wife, triumphantly. 'I thought as much! And if you have one secret then maybe you have others!'

'Oh, I don't have any secrets from you my dear.'

This went on for some time, and Assipattle was listening. After a while his father gave in and said, 'All right, I'll tell you the secret of Teetgong's speed. If I want him to stand still, I pat him on the left shoulder. If I want him to run fast, I pat him on the right shoulder, but if I want him to run as fast as the wind, I blow through a goose's thrapple (windpipe); I keep one in my coat pocket in case of emergencies.'

Once she had heard this she was contented and soon they were both fast asleep, snoring away merrily. Assipattle got up from the side of the fire and went over to where his father's coat was hanging. He took out the goose's thrapple and slipped silently outside and headed to the stable. When Teetgong saw him he started to neigh, rear up and kick, because this was not his master who was coming, but Assipattle gave him a pat on the left shoulder and he stood still. Assipattle got up on his back and gave him a pat on the right shoulder and away he ran, giving a loud neigh as he went. The sound of this woke up his father and he shouted to his sons to get horses and to ride after him.

'Stop! Thief!' they cried, because they didn't know that it was Assipattle.

After a short time his father was catching up, and he shouted, 'Hi, hi, ho! Teetgong, whoa!'

Teetgong stopped dead in his tracks, but Assipattle pulled out the goose's thrapple from his pocket and blew through it.

PAARP!

As soon as Teetgong heard the sound that it made he pricked up his ears and shot over the horizon, like an arrow from a bow. The old man and his sons gave up and turned their horses towards home. Assipattle clung on to Teetgong, who was well named, as in Orkney a Teetgong is a sudden gust of wind, and this horse could run as fast as any wind.

Eventually they came to a hill and down below them they saw a wide bay, and in that bay there was a big black island. However, it wasn't an island; it was the Stoor Worm's head. Assipattle rode down to the bay where he found a small house and went inside. There he saw an old woman lying asleep in her box bed with her grey cat curled up at her feet. The fire had been 'rested' for the night. In those days is was considered to be very bad luck to let your fire go out, as the luck of the house could go with it, so the fire was kept smouldering by putting damp peats on top of it. In the morning you just put some dry peats on top, gave it a puff with the bellows and away it would go. Assipattle took an iron pot from the side of the fire and he picked up a glowing peat with the fire tongs and put it into the pot and then ran outside.

Down by the shore he saw the king's boat with a guard standing in it and he was blue with cold.

'Hello,' said Assipattle, 'what like?'

'Cold!' grumbled the guard.

'Well, I'm just going to light a fire to boil some limpets for my breakfast; would you like to have a warm by my fire?'

'Better not,' said the guard, 'I can't leave my post or I'll get into trouble.'

'Better stay where you are then,' said Assipattle and he started to dig a hole, like he was making a hearth to shelter his fire in. Suddenly he started to shout, 'Gold! Gold! There's gold here!'

'Gold?' said the guard. 'Where?'

The guard jumped out of the boat and ran over to where Assipattle was, pushed him out of the way and started to dig in the ground like a dog. Assipattle picked up the pot with the peat in it, jumped into the king's boat, cast off the rope, hoisted the sail and was away across the bay before the guard knew what had happened. When he looked around he saw the king and his men arrive, just as the sun appeared over the horizon. As the first rays of the sun kissed the Stoor Worm's eyes it started to wake up and it gave the first of its seven great yawns. Assipattle positioned the boat alongside the monster's mouth so that when it yawned again the boat was carried into the Stoor Worm's mouth with the water that rushed inside and he went right down the Stoor Worm's throat. Down, down, deeper and deeper inside the Stoor Worm went Assipattle and the boat.

Now, I don't suppose that you are familiar with the internal plumbing of a stoor worm, so I had better explain. There was a large tunnel that ran right through the Stoor Worm, but here and there were smaller tunnels running off the big one and some of the water ran this way, some that way, until the water got shallower and shallower and the boat grounded. The inside of the monster glowed with a green, phosphorescent light, so Assipattle could easily see where he was going. He grabbed the pot with the peat in it and jumped out of the boat. Leaving the boat behind he ran and he better ran until he found what he was looking for; the Stoor Worm's liver! Well, you know how much oil there is in a fish's liver,

so imagine the amount of oil in the Stoor Worm's liver. It would be enough to solve our energy requirements forever. Assipattle took a knife from his belt with which he cut a hole in the Stoor Worm's liver. Into the hole he put the burning peat and he blew and he better blew until the oil spluttered into flames and then he ran back to his boat.

Meanwhile, back on the shore, the king was having a bad day. First he'd had to get up really early in order to fight the Stoor Worm and meet certain death (which would be enough to put me in a bad mood for the rest of the day) and then he arrived just in time to see some idiot steal his boat, sail across the bay and get swallowed by the Stoor Worm. Oh great! It just doesn't get any better than that, does it? As he stood by the shore, fuming with rage, one of his men said, 'Eh, Your Majesty, I've never seen the Stoor Worm do that before.'

'Do what?' snapped the king, looking the other way.

'Well, he's kind of – he's sort of – smoking.'

'Smoking?' shouted the king.

'Aye, well, look!'

And sure enough, when the king looked out over the bay he could see black smoke starting to billow out of the Stoor Worm's nose and out of its mouth. Now, the Stoor Worm started to feel sick and it spewed up all the water that was inside of it, which headed towards the shore as a huge wave. The king and his men, the old woman from the cottage with her cat and all the horses ran up the hillside to safety as the wave drew nearer, with Assipattle in his boat riding the crest of it. The boat was cast up high and dry right by the side of the king.

The thick, black smoke filled the sky and blocked out the sun, turning day into night. In its dying agony the Stoor Worm shot out its huge forked tongue so high that it caught hold of the moon. It would have pulled it from the sky, but the fork of its tongue slipped over the horn of the moon and it came back down to earth with a thundering crash, leaving a huge hole in the surface of the world. Water poured into the hole and it cut off the land of the Danes from Norway and Sweden. There it remains to this day as the Baltic Sea, and if you look at a map you can still see the great forks of the Stoor Worm's tongue.

The Stoor Worm's days were finally over. It rose its head up out of the sea in dying agony and it came back down to earth with a crash, which knocked out a lot of its teeth. These teeth fell into the sea and there they remain as the Orkney Islands. The head rose again and crash! More teeth were knocked out and these became Shetland. A third time the head rose and fell with a crash and more teeth were knocked out to make the Faroe Islands. Then the Stoor Worm curled up into a great big lump and died, and there it still remains; only now we call it Iceland. The flames that you see shooting out of the mountains there and the boiling water gushing out of the ground is caused by the Stoor Worm's liver, which is still burning.

The king took Assipattle in his arms and called him his son. He strapped the sword Sikkersnapper to his side and said, 'My boy, my kingdom is yours, as is my daughter, if she will have you.'

The Princess Gem de Lovely came over and as soon as she saw Assipattle she fell in love with him, because he was actually a very handsome young man, under all the ashes. The two of them were soon married and they reigned over the kingdom for many years and if they are not dead, then they are living yet.

You could well believe that story to be true if you have visited all the places created from the Stoor Worm's teeth. Orkney must be its incisors, as the islands are fairly flat. Shetland is formed from its premolars, higher and rugged, while the mountainous Faroe Islands are its molars, huge islands rising sheer from the sea to jagged points.

While Orkney is relatively flat it does have hills and even an island that is almost mountainous. Hoy, the 'High Island' of the Vikings, has round-topped hills that can be seen from many parts of Orkney. It lies to the south, like a rampart protecting the islands. There is a story of how the hills came into being.

The Caithness Giant

There was once a giant who lived in Caithness and there was nothing that he liked better than his garden. Although the earth where he lived was not too bad he looked north to Orkney with envious eyes. There he saw the green and fertile islands lying like emeralds in the sea and he coveted the dark, rich soil that lay there. One day he slung a straw basket on his back, took his staff in his hand, and waded across the Pentland Firth towards Orkney. He was so big that the water hardly came up to his knees. He stopped when he found a likely looking spot and he slung the straw basket onto the ground. With one of his huge hands he took a scoop of earth and dumped it into the basket, then with his other huge hand he took another huge scoop of earth and dumped it into the basket, filling it to the brim. He had left two great holes where he had taken the earth from and water ran into them, creating the Stenness and Harray Lochs. He slung the basket on his back and started on his journey home. As he went a huge lump of turf fell into the sea with a great splash, and there it remains to this day as the island of Graemsay. He had not got much further when suddenly, disaster struck! The straw rope that held his basket in place broke, spilling all his earth on the ground. The giant was so annoyed that he left it where it was and returned home, and there it remains as the Hills of Hoy.

In a slightly rude combination of the two stories already related, an old Orkney woman once remembered the story that she had heard as a child in the early twentieth century. A giant went to Norway to cut peats and he filled his basket and set off for home. As he waded through the sea he needed to answer the call of nature, so he dropped his trousers and, in her words, he 'shet land', and that was how Shetland was made. He carried on, but the strap of the basket broke and all his peats landed in the sea, and that's how Orkney was made. My apologies to my friends in Shetland, a place that I love very much, but I felt that this old story was worth recording for posterity, as it has never been written down before.

Any islander's life is dominated in one way or another by the sea; whether it's through ruined travel arrangements due to cancelled ferries or through empty supermarket shelves when lorries of food are stuck in Scotland. The sea rules our lives, but who rules the sea? Well, there is a very ancient story about that too.

◌⟋◌ THE MOTHER OF THE SEA ◌⟍◌

The old people of Orkney long held the belief in the Mother of the Sea. She was invisible to mortal eye, but everyone knew that she was there, protecting them. She was the spirit who controlled the sea during the summer months; an ancient goddess who calmed the waves and brought life and regeneration to all the creatures that lived in the sea. When the Mother of the Sea ruled, the fishermen's nets and creels were never empty. The seas were gentle and calm and people were safe to fish off the rocks or from their boats. It was a good time; a happy time of calm and plenty.

But the Mother of the Sea had an enemy. Teran was the spirit who ruled the sea in the winter time; a cold hearted, spiteful man who caused the storms that cast ships onto the jagged rocks that lie around the islands and made widows out of fishermen's wives. When he ruled there was nothing to be had in either net or creel, as fish, lobsters and crabs hid in deeper waters to avoid the turmoil of the waves.

During the summer months Teran was bound in chains at the bottom of the sea; a prisoner of the Mother of the Sea who gives life to all. But as the year waned so her powers diminished; sapped of her strength by giving life and controlling the waves. Then Teran would grow strong, break his fetters and the two spirits would fight. This occurred at the time of the Autumnal Equinox towards the end of September, and the storms that mark this point of the year are caused by their great struggle under the sea. Teran won and drove the Mother of the Sea from her realm; she would have to take up her abode on the earth during winter, passing unseen by human eye. Then was the time for the terrible reign of Teran when the sea boiled with rage. But as the spring started to draw near the Mother of the Sea grew once more in strength until, at the end of March, she returned to the sea and took up the battle once more with Teran at the Vernal Equinox. As they fought the sea was wild with fury and storms raged. Now it was Teran's turn to be overthrown, as his winter rage that drove the storms had in turn exhausted him. The Mother of the Sea bound him once more at the bottom of the sea and her reign began anew, bringing back life and calm to the sea once more. But as the year passed then Teran would once again break his bonds and regain control of the sea, and so it would be forever more until the end of time.

In Orkney a bad, wild person or animal was called a 'teran thing', but I'm not sure if there is a connection between the two. Quite likely there is. About twenty years ago a friend of mine told me that when he was a boy in Westray in the 1950s he had got himself a bamboo wand to go fishing off the rocks. On his way he passed my grandfather, Geordie Drever, who said to him, with a smile, 'Beuy, thoo haed better waatch oot that thoo disna catch the mither.'[1] He had no idea what Geordie meant by this, until he read the works of the nineteenth-century Sanday folklorist, Walter Traill Dennison, whose essays on Orkney folklore were virtually unknown at that time. My grandfather certainly wouldn't have had access to a printed version of the story, but maybe he knew it already.

It was once believed that there was a giant whale, called the 'Mester Whal' (the Great Whale), that lay far to the north, off the North Cape of Norway. The ebb and flow of the tide was said to be caused by the whale slowly breathing in and out. Another version of the Assipattle and the Stoor Worm story says that the Stoor Worm caused the tides by his breathing. In that version Assipattle is called Assipattie.

In the Pentland Firth lies the island of Stroma, to the north-east of which is the great whirlpool called the Swelkie, named 'the swallower' by the Vikings. It was believed that the Swelkie was caused by water pouring down through the eye of the giant quern stone, Grotti, turned day and night by the two giant women, Fenia and Menia. Grotti was a magic quern, which could grind whatever the owner wanted, so it grinds out salt at the bottom of the sea, which was its last owner's orders, and that is why the sea is salty. A little to the north, in the entrance to Scapa Flow, lies the small island of Swona. To the south of the island are whirlpools known as the Wells of Swona; this is how they came about.

✎ THE WITCH AND THE WELLS OF SWONA ✎

A long time ago there was a woman who lived on the island of South Ronaldsay who had the reputation of being a witch. She had fallen in love with a young man who lived locally and her heart burned for him. But the young man was not interested in her, for he was already in love with another. One day, as the young man was down by the shore, the witch came over to him and tried to persuade him to get into a boat that was lying there on the beach.

He refused, saying that he was there to meet his lover. The witch's heart filled with jealousy and a furious rage built up inside her, but she remained calm and smiled sweetly, as though nothing was wrong. When the young girl arrived the witch spoke sweet words to them; maybe she used her diabolical arts to bewitch them, but eventually she persuaded them to get into the boat with her and go for a row.

They left South Ronaldsay and headed west towards Swona. When they were nearing the island the witch suddenly used all her evil power and caused the boat to capsize, throwing them all into the water. The witch had nothing to fear, as her magic gave her the power to breathe underwater. However, the hapless young couple did not possess that skill and so the witch grabbed hold of the young man's arm, meaning to pull him out of the water and save him. The man held her arm in a vice-like grip, but he also grabbed the girl that he loved and would not let her go. They struggled for a short time before death took them, but still the dead man's hand held tight to the witch's arm. She struggled and twisted and turned wildly, trying to get free of them, but the harder she struggled the more entwined she became with their bodies and she could not break free from them. She is still there, under the sea, and she still struggles to be free of the dead, but they will not let go. Her twisting and turning causes the sea to form into whirlpools that are called the Wells of Swona, and that is her doom for all eternity.

✤ THE SAVILLE STONE ✤

There was once a witch who lived in Eday whose daughter was being courted by a young man whom the witch didn't approve of. She was forbidden to see him, but of course she still met him in secret. They decided to run away together so one night she slipped out of the house and ran to meet her lover, who had his boat ready by the shore. They sailed away before the witch woke up and realised what had happened. When she saw the boat away in the distance (for witches can see unusually far) she was so enraged that she picked up a huge boulder and threw it at them. She missed, and the stone landed in a field at Saville in Sanday and that's how the Saville Stone got there.

The truth behind this folk tale is even stranger than fiction. The Saville Stone is an erratic boulder carried to Orkney from Norway not by giants or witches but by a glacier during the last Ice Age. In 1879 work began to move the 14-ton rock 1 mile from its original position on the orders of the laird, Colonel Harwood, who wanted it as a feature in front of his house at Scar. A huge cart was built and a team of local crofters, including my great-grandfather Muir, managed somehow to lever it up onto the cart. Once there a team of twelve horses had to pull it up the brae. However, the physical exertion was too great and, in the words of my father, 'they sprang the horses' (they were ruptured with the effort). The cart remained near the top of the brae until the following summer when new horses were harnessed up to the giant cart and they pulled it the remaining distance. Only, not quite, for the cart broke under the weight of the rock a few hundred yards short of its destination and it has remained there ever since. The remains of the cart can be seen in old photographs and I once saw a wooden beam running under it one winter when the vegetation had died back and a rabbit hole had exposed it.

⚬ The Rainbow ⚬

The sky in Orkney is immense. With hardly any trees on the islands you can see from horizon to horizon, and the sheer scale of it is usually commented on by visitors to the islands. The quality of light is something special too, making it an inspirational place for artists and photographers. With a damp climate rainbows are a common sight; both single and double ones. I remember when I was working in North Ronaldsay in 1986 there was a very high tide and it was windy, yet the sun shone brightly. In the distance was Seal Skerry, a reef frequented by seals, which was usually above the water. That particular day the waves were blown over the top of the skerry and the spray that flew from them was caught by the sun and formed rainbows. Two or three moving arcs of colour crossed the top of the skerry; unbelievably beautiful. The Vikings called the rainbow Bifrost, the flaming bridge which linked the realm of the gods to that of mortals. If you saw a rainbow it meant that the gods were paying a visit.

The rainbow was believed to be the home of a group of beautiful female spirits called the 'keeries', who watched over the fate of those down below. If the end of a rainbow touched the chimney of a house it was said to be a bridge for a baby boy, and a keerie would bring one to be born in that house very soon. Baby girls, sadly, arrived unannounced. If both ends of a rainbow were seen to lie inside the hill dyke of a township, then it meant a death would occur there soon. Rainbows are beautiful, but you have to be able to read their hidden meanings.

THE MERRY DANCERS

The Northern Lights, called the Merry Dancers in Orkney, flicker in the winter skies. In Shetland they maintain the original form of the name, the Mirry Dancers; to 'mir' means to vibrate or tremble; this word is used in that sense in Orkney too.

Usually they are seen as curtains of green light, but once, when I was a young man of 20, I saw the whole northern skies lit up with curtains of coloured lights; red, blue, yellow and green. I was at Valdigar, where I was born, and had gone out on a frosty November night for a cigarette when I saw this most amazing spectacle. The curtains of light flickered and swayed, rising and falling like they were fanned by a gentle breeze. I have seen many beautiful things in the world, and have travelled far, but I have never seen anything quite as beautiful as that either before or since.

In Orkney it was believed that the Merry Dancers were just that, people dancing in the spirit world. They thought that in them they could see the souls of the dead joined together in a dance of joy. Some people swear that they have heard them as they swish by. One man in Sandwick thought that he could see his former laird from Stronsay amongst the dancers and he shouted to him to ask when he was going to be paid for the kelp that he had worked for him. With that the crowd of dancers disappeared, and he never did get his pay.

2

GIANTS AND DWARVES

As you can imagine, there are not that many stories about giants in Orkney as the gently undulating islands are too flat for them to hide in. That doesn't mean to say that there weren't any though. There are still places associated with them throughout the islands. On the small island of Wyre lived the most notorious of them all; Cubbie Roo. It has been said that he was based on an actual person who appears in the *Orkneyinga Saga*, a Norwegian chieftain called Kolbein Hruga who lived there in the mid-twelfth century. His nickname, 'Hruga', means 'heap' as he was said to be huge in stature. Large stones are pointed out in Evie, Rousay and Westray that were said to be missiles thrown by Cubbie Roo at other giants.

One man in North Walls (the eastern part of the island of Hoy) was out poaching rabbits one night when he saw a huge giant coming striding along. He got such a fright that he ran home and wouldn't go out for three weeks. He never went poaching again either.

✆ STANDING STONES ✆

Giants are associated with Neolithic standing stones and there are many stories attached to them. The solitary standing stone at Holland in North Ronaldsay, known locally as the Stan Stane, is 13ft high and has a small hole through it about 6ft from the ground. I once pondered if I could get my hand through the hole and came to the conclusion that I probably could, but getting it back again might prove more difficult. I didn't make the attempt. An old legend says that this stone once lay down by the shore, but an old giant woman saw it, stuck her finger right through it and carried it up onto the land and stuck it into the ground. It was once the focal point for revellers at New Year and young folk would meet there to play music and dance.

Other stones are also associated with giants and New Year, or more precisely, Hogmanay.[2] The Yetnasteen in Rousay leaves its usual place at the stroke of midnight on Hogmanay and in two jumps is down at the Loch of Scockness where it takes a drink before returning to the same spot for another year. The name Yetnasteen comes from the Old Norse *Jotunna-steinn*, meaning 'Giant's Stone'. The Watch Stone that stands by the bridge that crosses the narrow strait where the Stenness and Harray Lochs meet, also takes a drink at the stroke of midnight on Hogmanay. It is said that should anyone attempt to witness this stone taking its annual drink they will be prevented from doing so. Nothing bad will happen to them, but something will stop them from arriving on time. The Stone o' Quoybune in Birsay is a different kettle of fish though and has a distinctly darker side, as we will see later.

❧ THE SETTER STONE ❧

The massive Setter Stone in Eday is the largest standing stone in Orkney, standing 15ft high and measuring 7ft across at the base (which is much narrower than its upper part). Although it looks like a giant's hand, as weathering along fault lines in the stone has given it the impression of fingers, the story attached to it isn't about a giant but a laird. This laird wanted to erect this huge stone and so he had a deep pit dug. Earth was piled up and the stone was somehow balanced on top, but it wouldn't slide down into the hole. The laird called to his wife, who had a reputation for being very sharp tongued, and told her to stand on the end of the stone over the hole while they rocked it in order to get it to slide in. The laird's wife may have been a bit of a nag, but she wasn't stupid, and protested that it wasn't safe. The laird assured her that there was no danger and so she toddled off along the stone and started to jump up and down at the end. The laird and his men pushed the stone until it suddenly slid into the hole, with the laird's wife underneath it. The laird had always hated his wife and ordered his men to pull the stone upright and fill in the hole, and there she remains to this day.

⚬ THE STONE O' QUOYBUNE ⚬

One stormy night a ship was cast ashore in Birsay and its wreckage was scattered along the coastline. There was only one survivor; a young man who had managed to scramble ashore away from the sharp, jagged teeth of the rocks. He was more dead than alive when they found him, but the local folk carried him to a house where an old couple looked after him. Once he was warm again and had something hot in his belly he slept like a baby. He soon regained his strength and worked hard to help the old folk who had taken him in and given him shelter in his hour of need. But the year was wearing on, and Hogmanay was approaching. Nearby the house stood the Stone o' Quoybune and the old man warned the sailor that at the stroke of midnight, as the year changed, the stone would walk down to the Loch of Boardhouse to take a drink. He was warned that on no account must he try to see this happen as his life would be forfeited should he try. No one who had dared to watch the stone walk had lived to tell the tale. Well, the young man was bold and headstrong and he declared that he wasn't going to be frightened by a stone. He would watch it and let them know if the story was true or not. No matter how hard they tried to dissuade him he was determined that he would sit out all night to watch it.

When Hogmanay came the young sailor got ready for his night's vigil. Everyone else in the area shuttered their windows and barred their doors, but not the young sailor man. He strode over the field to the stone and, just to make absolutely sure, he climbed up to the top of it and sat there, waiting. What happened that night no one can say for sure, but the following morning they found his cold, dead body lying crushed at the foot of the stone.

ꙅꙩ The Dancing Giants ꙩꙅ

Long, long ago, there were giants in Orkney. They were big, loud, brash creatures, quarrelsome and slow witted, but they did love to dance. During the day they had to hide away, for the sun would see them and turn them into stone. They lived in fear of the yellow face, only coming out at night when the moon shone softly down on them.

One night they gathered at the place between the lochs to dance. A fiddler struck up a tune and the giants shouted with joy, linking hands and dancing around in a great big circle. Around and around they went as the fiddler played faster and faster. The sound of their feet as they danced must have sounded like thunder and felt like an earthquake as they sped around and around. They were having fun, in fact they were having so much fun that they completely forgot about the time. Suddenly, the sun rose above the horizon and caught them with its fiery eye. The music and the dancing stopped as each and every giant turned into stone. They are still there to this day, only now we call them the Ring of Brodgar.

The Comet Stone that stands in the field next to them was the fiddler; now silent in stone.

There is only one place in Orkney that is associated with the dwarves, and which bears their name. The Dwarfie Stane is a unique monument, a 28ft-long piece of rock, probably dumped there by the glacier that cut the valley. It was hollowed out in the Neolithic period to form a tomb and is thought to be the only rock-cut tomb in the UK. Inside are two chambers, resembling stone beds with a sill in front of them. One has a rounded area carved into the wall. Outside lies a stone that was once used to seal the doorway. A hole in the roof, now filled in, shows where it was broken into, probably in prehistory. In the 1560s, when it is first mentioned, the doorway was still sealed and the hole in the roof was in existence, although no one knew anything about it. The inland cliff next to it is called the Dwarfie Hammars, from the Old Norse *Hamarr*, meaning a crag jutting out of a hillside. The nearby valley is called Trowieglen, after the trows, or fairy folk. It is said that if you go into Trowieglen then you will lose something, for the trows will steal it. The story relating to the Dwarfie Stane is one of the earliest Orkney folk tales ever written down, being recorded by Jo Ben in the 1560s. He claims that the stone was the abode of giants, although they must have been very small giants to have fitted inside. Much more likely that it was in fact the home of a dwarf, as the name implies.

☜ THE DWARFIE STANE ☞

There was once a dwarf who lived in Hoy with his wife. His wife was pregnant and so he set about making a fine new home for them both. He found a fine big stone and set about hollowing it out to form a comfortable home for a dwarf and his wife. He cut their beds into the wall, complete with stone pillows and a curving wall in his wife's bed to accommodate her swollen belly. Soon his fine new home was ready and the two of them went inside to admire his handiwork. Dwarves love to be inside rocks, so they felt very comfortable indeed.

Happy as these two dwarves were, trouble was not far from their door, for there was another dwarf who lived in Hoy and he grew jealous of the pair and their new home. He plotted and schemed about what he could do to get rid of them and steal their house. Eventually he waited until they had gone to bed one night and he stood on the Ward Hill with a sling. He had made a stone that exactly fitted the doorway and he put it into his sling, whirling it around and around his head before flinging it at the dwarves' new home. The stone hit the doorway, right on target, and sealed it tightly shut. All he had to do now was to wait a while until he knew that they were dead and then cut out the stone and take the house for himself. But dwarves are very strong and when the dwarf inside found that the stone in the doorway wouldn't budge he took his hammer and started to strike the ceiling with it until he had

knocked a hole through the roof. He crawled outside and saw his
rival standing on the hillside, sling in hand, and his blood boiled.
He set off after him and chased him all over Hoy. In fact, he might
be chasing him yet!

I have heard a different version of this story, but I can't vouch for it.
It said that a dwarf lived in the stone and one day a giant saw him
working inside the stone and he took a rock and shoved it into the
doorway to trap him inside. The giant chuckled to himself when
he heard the dwarf muttering inside and he bent over the stone to
hear him better. The dwarf, who was very strong, took his thumb
and stuck it right through the top of the stone, creating a hole and
sending a sharp piece of rock flying upwards into the air. This piece
of rock hit the giant in the head, fatally wounding him. The giant
staggered away some distance before falling down dead, where his
petrified body can still be seen to this day. This large piece of rock
is now called the Patrick Stone, but I don't know how it came by
that name.

3

TROWS, FAIRIES
AND HOGBOONS

In Orkney there is a great deal of confusion about the types of supernatural mound-dwelling creatures that occupy the islands. The term 'trow' is usually applied to them; the name has been explained as being from the same source as the Norwegian troll. But the term 'fairy' is also used to describe similar creatures. It seems to be a mixture of Old Norse and Celtic beliefs, with a pinch of something uniquely Orcadian to give it zest. Both the trows and fairies live in mounds, often conspicuous artificial ones that cover Neolithic tombs or Iron Age brochs, but also mounds that were formed naturally as rocks and clay was deposited by glaciers at the end of the Ice Age. These mounds were treated with fear and were not disturbed by our ancestors, which resulted in the excellent preservation of many ancient monuments. To dig into them or remove them was a dangerous thing to do and could result in the sudden death of a farmer's livestock or even family members. Trows and fairies would carry off newborn babies, leaving changelings in their place, as well as stealing cattle, horses or whatever took their fancy.

Just to confuse things further, many people associated the trows and fairies with the Picts, the late Iron Age occupants of Orkney whose culture was destroyed or swamped by that of the Vikings. Ancient structures from any period were given the name 'Picts Hooses'[3] and it seems that the name was applied

to the supernatural dwellers inside these mounds. My great-grandmother, who lived at the croft of North Tuan in Westray in the late nineteenth century, used to make very fine, strong home-brewed ale, which my great-grandfather used to kindly drink for her. When he had one of his old pals by one night (a retired sea captain, I believe) they did great service to the ale so that when the old boy staggered homewards he claimed that he could see the Picts dancing on top of a nearby mound.

✎ THE ROUSAY CHANGELING ✎

A Rousay couple had a baby boy, their first child, and he was the apple of their eye. They loved that baby so much, fussing over him and cuddling him while he would gurgle and coo with delight.

All was happiness and joy; until the day he changed. Who knows what happened, maybe they got careless and left the boy unattended while they went to fetch something from outside, which was a dangerous thing to do. Babies had to be watched for the first while and never left alone, especially before they were christened, or the fairies could steal them. A knife and a Bible were usually left in the cradle as protection, as the fairy folk cannot stand either of those things and have no power to cause harm if the baby is protected in that way. But their baby boy started to cry and wail and he grew thinner and thinner, wasting away in front of their very eyes. He ate well, but was never contented and he never put on weight. Quite the opposite, in fact.

Things got so bad that the mother sent word to an old woman who lived in the district to come and see her. She was regarded as a wise woman; a person who could see the things that were usually hidden from others. When the wise woman arrived the mother took her to the cradle to see her baby. There he lay, a poor wizened creature with wild staring eyes whose cries sent a shiver down your spine. The woman looked at him and then went away, followed by the mother.

'That is not your son,' said the wise woman, 'that is a fairy changeling. They have come and taken your baby and replaced it with one of their own.'

'What can I do to get my boy back?' asked the mother.

'You have to be brave, if you mean to win back your son. You must take a steel wedge and a bible and go up the hill to Muckle Water, beyond that you will see a rock face that has a crack running right down it. Take the steel wedge and drive it into that crack and the wall will open. Inside you will see a fairy woman; you must strike her three times in the face with the Bible. On no account must you utter a sound while you are in there, or all will be lost. Once you've hit her three times turn around and walk out, without looking back. If you do not follow these instructions faithfully, then you will never see your son again. Do you understand?'

'Yes, I understand.'

The mother took a Bible and a steel wedge that was used for splitting rocks in the quarry and began to walk up the steep hill towards Muckle Water. The wind rippled the surface of the water as she walked on towards the rocky outcrops. There she saw the rock face with a crack running down it and she forced the steel wedge into it. Slowly, the rock face opened to reveal a fine hall inside the hill. Sitting on a chair inside the hall was a fairy woman with the stolen baby on her knee. The fairy shouted at the woman and tried everything that she could to trick her into talking, but the mother remained silent. Her heart burned for her baby boy and she had to force herself not to grab him and hold him tight to her breast, as this would ruin all hope of saving him. Instead, she looked into the eyes of the fairy who had stolen her child and saw the cold fire that burned within them. She raised the Bible and struck it against the fairy woman's face, who screamed so loud that it seemed that the walls would crumble. Again the mother struck her in the face with the Bible, and then a third time, before silently turning and walking out the door without looking back. The woman ran down the slope, past the loch and headed home. Her heart was beating so wildly and loudly that it was all that she could hear. Onward she ran until she reached her house and burst through the door, gasping for breath and with tears streaming down her face. And there he was, lying soundly asleep in the cradle, her own baby boy, returned to her.

THE TROWS OF TROWIEGLEN

Rackwick in Hoy is one of those special places in the world, not only very beautiful but with a certain atmosphere that you just can't describe in words. It is a valley that lies between two high hills and faces south across the Pentland Firth; the home of crofter fishermen who tilled the soil and risked their lives at sea to put food on the table. A sandy beach lies beneath a ridge of round boulders, each stone striped with different colours as if a giant had spilled a bag of boiled sweets there long ago, in the time of legends. At either side of the bay rise high, straight-sided cliffs of red sandstone, stained blood-like by the rays of the setting sun. It is truly a magical place, steeped in mystery and an inspiration for musicians, poets and painters over the years.

Mansie Ritch was a young man who lived in Rackwick. One day he set off to walk over the hills to Longhope, where he had some business to attend to, only beginning the return journey as the day was wearing on. In the summertime it never really gets dark, but Mansie was still keen to get to the safety of his home before the end of the day. This journey took him past the Trowieglen, a place that Mansie was keen to avoid at the best of times. As he approached it he suddenly started to feel strange; he was still walking but his legs seemed to be striding along by themselves, against his will. He felt drawn towards the Trowieglen, an irresistible urge to venture into that magical realm of the trows. He couldn't fight it, so he gave in to it and let himself be drawn towards the head of the glen. Then he saw that he was not alone, for a crowd of peedie[4] folk, no bigger than a foot tall, were walking alongside him in a procession, all going in the same direction.

As they went deeper into the Trowieglen Mansie saw a light in front of them, about halfway down the glen. It seemed to be coming from the opening of a cave in its rocky walls. When he reached the cave entrance the procession stopped and the trow who was leading it told him that he could not enter their realm without a written pass, signed by 'Himself'. He told him to wait there until he saw if Himself would see him. Mansie was feeling scared by this time, but his curiosity had got the better of him and he wanted to see what lay inside and who this person was that they called 'Himself'. After about five minutes a trow

came to the door and beckoned to Mansie to
come inside. Mansie was shaking with fear by
this time, but he didn't want the trows to see
that he was scared so he drew himself up to
his full height and went inside the cave. To his
amazement Mansie found himself not in a cave
but in a beautifully decorated hall. Brilliantly
coloured tapestries were hung on the walls
and a soft carpet was under his feet. Expertly
carved furniture was everywhere and in the
distance Mansie could see that a dance was
in full swing.

Mansie was led into a small side chamber
and was told to wait. Then in came Himself;
he was a bit bigger than the other trows, being
about 18in tall, with a long, pointed white beard
and dressed in a suit of pale blue velvet clothes
with a blue turban on his head. Two trows came in
carrying a throne for Himself to sit down on.

'So,' said Himself, 'do you know who
I am?'

'No,' said Mansie, trying to sound brave,
'I don't know who you are, but I'm not scared
of you either.'

The peedie man rocked backwards in his chair, roaring with
laughter.

'Well said, Mansie my boy, well said! I am Himself, and I'm the
head child here in the Trowieglen. You cannot come into my realm
unless you have a piece of paper with my name upon it. But I will
sort that out for you, easy enough. Tell me, Mansie, would you
care to join me in a drop of heather ale?'

Mansie started to feel more at home now, especially at the offer
of the trow's magical ale.

'Yes, thank you,' he said, 'I would like that very much.'

Himself ordered the ale and trow servants brought them both a cog⁵ of foaming heather ale. Mansie drank down the ale and declared that he had never tasted such a good brew in his life before. As he drank he could feel himself getting as light as air. Then Himself invited him to join in the dance.

Mansie went into the main hall where the dance was taking place. All the peedie trow women were dressed in white and Mansie thought that it was the most beautiful sight that he had ever seen. He didn't know the dances, but he tried to join in anyway, much to the delight of the trows who clapped and cheered as he skipped around. They danced and laughed with not a care in the world and Mansie thought that he had never been happier in his life than at that time. As the dancing continued Mansie felt more at home than ever, until he began to think that he could do with a smoke.

'Would you mind, sir, if I have a smoke?' Mansie asked Himself.

'A smoke?' said Himself, obviously puzzled by the request. 'What do you mean "a smoke"?'

Mansie took out his clay pipe and a twist of strong tobacco. He took a piece, rubbed it until it was loose and then filled his pipe. Himself and all the other trows gathered around in amazement, for they had never seen the like of this before. Then he struck a light and lit the tobacco, throwing his head back and blowing out a large cloud of smoke into the air. All of a sudden the trows began to cough and splutter and to fall on the floor. Mansie was powerless to prevent the disaster that was unfolding around him as one by one the trows fell to the ground in a dead faint. The last one to succumb to the smoke was Himself and as he fell over everything went dark. The next thing that Mansie knew was when he woke up in front of a rabbit hole in Trowieglen with not a trow in sight.

∽ MANSIE O' FEA ∾

Mansie o' Fea lived in Sandwick a long, long time ago. He had a reputation of being a strange man who was in league with the fairies. Not only was he said to be in league with the fairies he was actually supposed to be married to one, having two wives at once; a mortal one and a fairy one. Whenever his fairy wife called to spend the night with him her mortal rival would fall into a deep sleep from which she could not be roused until her fairy rival was gone. Mansie had three daughters with his fairy wife and she taught him many things that he found useful in later life. When one farmer came to see him, saying that his horse was ill and seemed to be wasting away, it only took him one look to know that the fairies were taking it at night and riding it so hard that it was dying of exhaustion. He advised that the farmer bar the stable door with a strong piece of wood which had a Bible fastened to it and that would prevent the fairies from interfering with his horse, and so it did.

Mansie suffered a double tragedy as both his mortal and his fairy wife died. He married a second mortal wife which proved to be a disaster. She spent what money he had and made his life a misery with her constant nagging. Mansie took to the booze as an escape, which did not improve domestic harmony. One day he went off to a 'change house', an establishment with a licence to sell beer (and with a drop of home-made whisky and some smuggled Dutch gin under the counter, away from prying eyes). Mansie was gone for a long time and his wife was getting anxious so she sent a servant boy to look for him. A search of the Sandwick pubs eventually bore fruit in the shape of a rather plastered Mansie. The boy managed to persuade him to go home and led him outside to where his horse was tied. Mansie climbed up into the saddle and the boy jumped up behind him. They set off at good speed on the road home. Mansie asked the boy if he had ever seen the fairies before, to which the boy replied that he had not. Mansie then asked him if he would like to see the fairies, to which the boy said yes, he would like to see them. So Mansie set his foot on top of the boy's foot and as soon as he had done that the boy saw that they were surrounded by fairies on horseback who were driving a cow before them in the direction of the Bay of Skaill. Mansie explained that the cow had come from the farm of Bain and that the fairies had left one of their own dead cows in the byre in place of it. In the morning George Marwick would find one of his cows lying dead without realising that it had been changed by the fairies. And so it came to pass, just as Mansie o' Fea had said.

✑ The Fiddler and the Trow ✑

The parish of Deerness is attached to the rest of the East Mainland of Orkney by a thin strip of sand. At the west end of that sandy thread lies the great mound of Dingieshowe[6], used by the Vikings to hold their 'thing' assemblies where laws were made and disputes settled.

Tam Bichan was the finest fiddle player in all of Deerness, some said that he was the best in all of the broken isles of Orkney. Whenever there was a wedding or a party Tam was the first to be invited. One day Tam took a walk down to the sand at Dingieshowe and started to play the fiddle. He did it just for the sheer love of playing and for no other reason, but it proved to be a very dangerous thing to do, for two reasons. First, it was Midsummer's Day, and the trows have their greatest powers at Midsummer and Midwinter. Secondly, he was standing on the shoreline between high and low water. This was a place where the Devil and all supernatural creatures had great power because it is neither a part of the land nor a part of the sea, for sometimes it is covered with water and sometimes it is dry. There Tam stood, below the tide mark on Midsummer's Day and playing his finest set of reels and jigs.

Tam soon noticed that he wasn't alone, for he saw someone about the size of a 5 year old coming towards him. But it was the funniest-looking 5 year old that Tam had ever seen. He looked ancient with long, grey hair and long grey whiskers, bushy eyebrows with dark, twinkling, mischievous eyes. Tam knew that his fiddle playing had attracted a trow.

'Well Tam,' said the trow, 'that was very fine playing.'

'Thank you,' said Tam, for he knew that you had to be polite with the peedie folk.

'Tell me Tam, would you be good enough to play for me and my friends tonight. We are having a party to celebrate the time of the year.'

Tam was not the sort of man to refuse the offer of a party and he accepted. The trow led him up the beach and towards the great mound of Dingieshowe. To Tam's amazement there was a door standing open in the side of the mound and he followed the trow inside. Down and down they went, deep into the heart of the mound. Inside was a large room all ready for the dancing; it had nothing in it except a large barrel standing at one end.

'Jump up on the barrel Tam and take a seat,' said the trow, so Tam did as he was told.

'Would you care for a drop to drink Tam?'

'Oh, yes, I'd love a drop of something,' said Tam.

The trow filled a cog with a golden-coloured drink from the barrel that Tam was sitting on and handed it to him.

'Try that; it's heather ale. You'll never have tasted anything as good as that before.'

Sure enough, the heather ale was delicious and Tam could feel its warm glow going down his throat and filling his whole body. His nose started to tingle, his fingers started to tingle, his toes started to tingle, and maybe a few other places tingled too, but it's not that sort of story! Tam picked up his fiddle and he started to play. He had never played better in his whole life and the music that flowed from the fiddle was as intoxicating as fine wine. The trow started to dance and soon he was joined by other trows who danced, until the room was full of them, all dancing and laughing and drinking heather ale. The fun went on all night, but by its end Tam was starting to feel tired and he wanted to go home to his bed. He said goodbye to the trow, who thanked him, saying, 'You are very welcome to come back anytime you want, Tam. But, remember to bring your fiddle with you.'

Tam started to walk up the long passage that led to the outside world and out through the door. He yawned, stretched, then looked behind him to see that the door had gone; there was nothing there but grass blowing on the side of the mound. As he started to walk home Tam started to notice that things were somehow not quite right. There was a house over there that he didn't recognise and a haystack where there hadn't been one yesterday. Things were the same, but not quite right. Tam thought that it was just because he was tired and he had had rather a lot of heather ale, but when he turned down the road that led to his own house he got the shock of his life, for there stood his home in ruins. The thatch on the roof was gone and the windows stood empty of glass. He ran inside and shouted for his mother, but there was no reply. He didn't know what had happened and he wandered around aimlessly until he saw a boy on the road. Tam shouted to him, 'Hey, you there. What has happened to that house and what happened to the old woman who lived there?'

'I don't know,' said the boy, 'you had best come home with me and talk to my father.'

Tam followed the boy back to his house and went in where an elderly man was eating his breakfast. When Tam came in the man went as white as a sheet and said, 'Tam Bichan; is that you boy?'

'Yes, I'm Tam Bichan, but I'm sorry, I don't know who you are.'

'Don't you recognise me Tam? I'm Andrew Delday.'

'You can't be Andrew Delday, you're far too old.'

'I don't know about me being too old, but Tam, I'm thinking that you are too young!'

'Too young? What do you mean?'

'Well Tam, you've been away for a long time.'

'No I haven't,' said Tam, whose head was spinning, 'I've only been away for a night.'

'Ah, it's been longer than a night. Now let me think. Yes; it was fourteen years and a day since we last saw you. You were seen heading down to the beach at Dingieshowe with your fiddle, but you never came back. We thought that you must have fallen into the sea and been swept away. We did search for your body, but we never found you. Your mother was an old woman and when she passed away the croft was never let again and the storms blew off the roof and knocked in the windows.'

Tam couldn't believe it; he thought that he was only away for a night, but time passes at a different rate when you are with the trows. The news of Tam's return spread like wildfire around Deerness. He was back and not looking a day older than when he left. They said that the very cap on his head was the same. He was asked to play the fiddle once again, but he never played in public any more. It was said that when folk went past the house where he then lived they could hear him playing strange tunes that they had never heard before. But Tam could not settle down and avoided company, until one day he was seen walking down towards Dingieshowe with his fiddle in his hand and he was never seen again. They do say that if you go to the great mound at Dingieshowe on Midsummer night and you listen closely at the side of the mound you can hear the sound of a fiddle playing and a party in full swing.

☙ THE TROW SERVANT ❧

There was once a farmer in the West Mainland who had a very strange servant, for he had a trow working for him. The trow had agreed to work for nothing more than a plate of porridge for his supper every night. The bowl of porridge was left on the kitchen table before the family went to bed and it was empty in the morning.

The farmer had fallen for the charms of a young woman from the town of Kirkwall and the two were married. She was a kind-hearted young woman and she sometimes saw the trow going about his work and wearing the same old worn-out clothes, summer and winter. On a cold winter's day she thought that the biting north wind must blow through the holes in his clothes and that he must be miserably cold. She decided that, as he was such a hard worker, then he deserved to be given some new clothes. She set about making him a little suit from home-spun cloth with a waistcoat, woollen stockings, a little hat with a buckle on the front and even a nice pair of children's boots that she thought would fit him, which she polished until they shone like black diamonds. She left the clothes on the table next to his bowl of porridge and then went to bed.

After she had been asleep for a short time she and her husband were woken by the most tremendous shouts coming from the kitchen, 'Yahoo! Yeehee! Yippee!!'

They both ran to the kitchen to see what was going on and they saw the trow standing there, dressed in his fine new clothes.

'See me?' he said. 'I'm a gentleman now. I'm far too good to work for the likes of you!'

And with that the trow walked out the door, left the farm and was never seen again. The deal had been broken, as the trow was given clothes as well as his porridge. The farmer always cursed his wife's good heart as she had cost him the finest and cheapest servant that he ever had.

The Death of the Mainland Fairies

The fairies on the Orkney Mainland had had enough. A terrible plague had swept the island, bringing fear and misery in its wake. As far as they were concerned the awful plague was not a disease, it was much worse than that; it was ministers! In every church the ministers rang bells and sang hymns, they blessed the people and cursed the fairies. In the end the fairies couldn't stand it anymore and they decided that something must be done. They had a meeting and decided that the Mainland was no longer a suitable place for them to live and that they needed a wilder, less populated place where they could live in peace. Their eyes turned towards the hills of Hoy and smiles crossed their faces. Yes; they would go and live in Hoy where there were still empty places away from prayers and psalms. They made their plans and then returned to their mounds.

On the next night when the moon was full they all gathered at the Black Craig in Stromness, bringing with them a simman rope made of twisted straw. The most agile of the fairies took an end of the straw rope and leapt right over the Hoy Sound and landed on the other side. He secured the rope on Hoy while the others secured their end on the Black Craig. Using the rope like a bridge they all started to run surefootedly towards Hoy. However, when they were only halfway across disaster struck and the rope broke.

All the Mainland fairies fell into the strong currents of the Hoy Sound and were swept out into the Atlantic Ocean and drowned. The solitary survivor, standing on Hoy, howled like a dog when he saw this. He threw himself into the cold, dark waters and was swept away with the rest of them. Soon he too sunk beneath the waves and that was the end of the Mainland fairies.

Hogboons, or Hog Boys, are similar to trows, but they are not related. They live in mounds as well, but they are attached to a family and will bring you good luck and prosperity as long as you share your produce with them. If you pour milk or ale over the mound then they are happy. Put butter, cheese or ground corn on top of the mound and all will be well for the family; but should you neglect the hogboon then you are playing a dangerous game. A hogboon ignored grows bitter and angry and will make your life a misery.

It is thought that the hogboon is the guardian spirit for the family and that it is the spirit of the farmer who originally broke out the land. When James Farrar MP excavated the great Neolithic tomb of Maeshowe in 1861 he was warned by local people that he should leave it well alone, as a powerful spirit called the Hog Boy lived inside it and that it possessed great strength.

The Hogboon of Hellihowe

In the north-east corner of the parish of Burness in Sanday lies the house of Hellihowe. A great mound stood near the house and in this mound there lived a hogboon. The family used to tend the hogboon faithfully, sharing the produce of the croft with its guardian spirit so that they enjoyed every success. The cattle had fine, healthy calves, the sheep all had twin lambs, the crops grew well and gave plenty of grain. Everything went well, as long as the hogboon received its share. But the crofter married a woman who knew nothing about the hogboon so, when her husband tried to leave food out for it, she scolded him and the hogboon got nothing to eat.

One night, after not being fed again, the hogboon decided to go into the house to see what the matter was. Maybe there was sickness in the house, he thought, and all the poor people were too ill to go out to the mound with food. But when he got inside he saw them all sleeping soundly with not a care in the world. He was not too happy about this, but he thought that he could at least get a bite of porridge from the pot by the side of the fire. When he looked into the pot he saw to his annoyance that it was empty; not only was it empty but it had been scraped clean. Nothing was left for him to eat. Rage burned inside him at their neglect and he swore that they would suffer for this. And so it came to pass, for the crop failed and the cattle wouldn't thrive and the sheep ran off.

Not only that, but if the family tried to do anything they found the tool that they needed was missing, they were the butt of practical jokes and everything went wrong.

One day the crofter went to see the laird, hoping that they could get another croft and start a new life for themselves. He was in luck, as the laird had just the place for him, and better still, it was a long way away from Hellihowe. The crofter returned home with the happy news for his wife. They borrowed horses with pack saddles and started to fasten their meagre belongings to them, at least, the belongings that the hogboon had not broken or hidden. To the saddle of the first horse they tied their plout kirn[7], then all the other smaller articles. Once they were ready they left Hellihowe and set off for their new home. As they got further and further away they felt happy, hoping that their new life would be better without the constant attacks from the spiteful hogboon. At last they saw their new home before them, the crofter was so happy that he started to whistle a merry tune. Suddenly, the lid flew off the plout kirn and the hogboon stuck out his head and said, 'We're getting a good day for the flitting, Goodman!'[8]

What the crofter had forgotten was that a hogboon doesn't go with the land, it goes with the family.

4

MERMAIDS

Orkney folk of times long gone believed in a race of creatures called the fin folk that lived on vanishing islands called Hilda-Land or under the sea in the fine city of Finfolkaheem. It was said that their womenfolk were the mermaids and that these mermaids were always on the lookout for a human husband. This was because if they married a fin man then they would lose their great beauty and become hideous crones called fin wives, who would make a living on land as witches. If a mermaid married a human husband then she would keep her beautiful looks for all eternity, once they had consummated the union.

Some folklorists claim that mermaids and selkie folk are one and the same creature. I strongly disagree. Maybe in some places the two have become confused, but not in Orkney. The great nineteenth-century folk tale collector, Walter Traill Dennison (1825–1894), was very clear about this. Writing in 1892 he said:

Karl Blind[9], in the *Contemporary* for September 1881, speaks of the mermaid as assuming the form and wearing the skins of seals. Now this view would have been regarded as utterly heterodox by the old Orkney peasantry whom I knew forty years ago. To them the idea of a mermaid wearing a sealskin would have seemed as ridiculous as if some blundering newspaper should state that, 'Yesterday Her

Majesty the Queen held a Drawing Room, dressed in a coat of chain armour.'

In the same article a Shetland correspondent had written that, 'Such an idea as a Mermaid I never heard of till I saw it in some English work of fiction.' Dennison responded:

My experience in Orkney is exactly the reverse of that of the Shetlander. And I have heard a hundred times more about Mermaids from the lips of the Orkney peasants than I ever saw in books.

As Dennison was a Sanday man I would love to think that some of these 'Orkney peasants' from whom he heard his stories may have been my ancestors. He goes on to say that while both men and women believed that the mermaid possessed a tail when in the water, the women believed the tail to be a petticoat, embroidered with silver and gold, that was tied around the feet while swimming, but left open to reveal dainty feet when on land, but the men said it was a part of her body. Denison recorded the story of how this tail came into being.

⚭ HOW THE MERMAID GOT HER TAIL ⚭

The mermaid was the first to be created and the most beautiful, although in the beginning she didn't have a tail. Way back, when the world was young, there was a great queen who lived on Earth; some say that it was Eve herself. One day she went for a swim and was just leaving the water when she saw a beautiful creature sitting on a rock, combing her long, golden hair. It was like a woman, only much more beautiful, and her song was so sweet that it dripped with magic and enchantment. Eve was amazed, but she also felt jealous of the beauty of this woman who sat there naked in the sunlight, so she sent one of her servants over to her with the gift of a dress to wear. The woman looked at the dress, smiled, and shook her head. She replied in song:

I am the queen o' the sea, and mermaid's me neem,
Tae shaw me fair body I dinno tink sheem,
Nae claiths fil me skin, nae dress will I wear
But the braw taets o me bonnie, bonnie hair.[10]

Eve was furious at the dismissive response of the mermaid and she and all the other women protested most vehemently that something had to be done about her. In their eyes the mermaid was so unbelievably beautiful and shameless that no man would ever want a mortal woman again. The bitter protests were heeded and the mermaid was doomed to wear a fish's tail. However, the men felt sorry for her and they managed to help her to avoid this awful fate. If the mermaid could get a mortal man to fall in love with her then she had the power to lay aside her tail forever, as long as she was with him. That is why mermaids are still so keen to win for themselves a mortal husband, so that they can again be as beautiful as they once were.

❦ The Mermaid Bride ❦

Johnny Croy was the most handsome man in all of Sanday, if not the whole of Orkney. Many a young lass gazed on him with hungry eyes as he passed by, but he was a shy young man and if he noticed their looks then he never let it show.

Sanday, as the name implies, is a flat island with beaches of white sand that stretch for miles. One day Johnny was out by the cliffs at the south-west of the island, where the sandy land rises and the selkies play, looking for driftwood for the fire or to make things with. Suddenly he heard a more beautiful sound than he had ever heard in his whole life before. Music was being carried towards him on the warm, summer's breeze; a song as intoxicating as strong, sweet perfume. It filled his senses until his head was spinning like he was about to faint. Johnny braced himself for a moment, fighting the enchantment of this song, but the urge to see where it was coming from was too great and he moved forward, slowly, among the stones and seaweed that formed the beach. Then he saw her. He stood fixed to the spot like a statue as he stared in wonder at the most beautiful woman he had ever seen in his whole life. The mermaid sat on a rock in the sun, combing her long, golden hair with a comb of pure gold. She was naked from the waist up, but wore a petticoat of silver, shot through with blues and greens, which was twisted together to form a tail. She sang as she combed her hair and her song drew him to her like a moth to a flame. Johnny swore at that moment that he would never take a bride unless it was this mermaid; his heart was filled with love for her and desire burned within him like the sun.

The mermaid had not seen him, so completely was she lost in her song. Johnny realised that he must act fast, but what was he to do? He crouched down on the beach, crawling among the rocks and seaweed like an animal until he was between her and the sea. She still had not seen him when he was within striking distance and then, with a lunge, he grabbed her tightly and kissed her on the lips. The mermaid sat there for a moment, stunned, but then she swept up her tail and hit him on the side of the head, sending him sprawling among the rocks. She gathered up her petticoat and ran down to the sea and plunged into the water. Now it was Johnny's turn to be stunned as he gathered his senses together and shook his head. He was impressed at her strength, as no man had ever been strong enough to put him on his back before. He saw that she was in the sea, just off shore, and she stared at him with smouldering eyes. She was furious with him for having so rudely

kissed her without asking her permission, but mixed in with that anger there was love at the sight of this handsome man.

It was then that Johnny noticed something at his feet, glinting in the sunlight. He saw that it was her golden comb lying among the seaweed. He picked up the comb and held it aloft for her to see and said, 'Thank you for leaving me this token of your love.'

'My comb!' cried the mermaid. 'Give it back to me; please! I cannot go back to my home under the sea without my comb; I would be mocked and laughed at. Oh, my handsome man, please give it back to me.'

'No, no, my pretty maid,' said Johnny, 'I will only give this back to you if you promise to marry me and come and live with me on land. I have a fine farm at Volyar with a good stock of cattle and sheep.'

'No, I couldn't live in your cold land, with your black rain and white snow. I couldn't bear your icy wind and frost, and your smoky fires would dry me up like the poor fishes that you hang over it. No; come with me to Finfolkaheem, our home under the sea where mermaids and fin folk dwell in peace and happiness. There is no wind or rain in my land, and you will rise in power and wealth and become an important man. We will live in joy and happiness forever more.'

They argued like this, back and forth, for some time with neither one wanting to back down. As they talked Johnny and the mermaid fell more deeply in love with each other, but their conversation was interrupted by the sight of someone in the distance walking towards them. The mermaid turned and swam away, lamenting the loss of her comb. Her golden hair was streaming over her white back like sunbeams glinting on snow. Johnny turned around and walked back to his home at Volyar with a heavy weight of sorrow hanging about his heart.

When Johnny's mother saw him coming along the road she could see that something was wrong. When she asked him what the matter was he took out the mermaid's golden comb that he had been clutching to his heart and showed it to her. She stared at it with a look of horror on her face, for she had the reputation of being a wise woman who knew what others didn't. Johnny told her all about the mermaid and his love for her and how he could never be happy unless he had her for his bride. His mother frowned, saying, 'You are a fool for falling in love with a sea lass, but what can you expect from a man? If you want my advice you will go back to the shore, throw that comb as far out into the sea as you can and forget all about her.'

'That I cannot do, mother.'

'Aye, you are a right gappus[11] indeed! Well, if you insist on having a sea lass as your bride then you must do as I tell you. You must keep that comb in your possession, for as long as you have it you have power over her. She won't rest until she gets it back. Then you will be able to bend her will to yours. But, for God sake boy, if you have any spark of wit in your head you will return it to the sea, for no good will come of this.'

'That is my concern; but I cannot live without her.'

So the time passed slowly for Johnny Croy. The days dragged by and the nights seemed endless. Sleep scarcely visited Johnny as he tossed and turned in his bed; his mind burning with the vision of the mermaid's beauty. One morning as dawn approached, and the night was darkest, Johnny fell into a fitful sleep. In his dreams he could hear the song of the mermaid filling his head. So sweet, so beautiful, so full of enchantment. Then his eyes opened, but the song continued; his room was filled with that wonderful voice, for there at the foot of his bed sat the mermaid.

'Hello, my handsome man. I have come to ask you if you will return my comb.'

'No, I will not do that.'

'Then come with me, and be my loving husband in Finfolkaheem. You will live in a castle of crystal and be with me forever more.'

'No, my sweet love. Marry me; be my bride and live with me here.'

'I will make you an offer, which I think is fair. I will marry you, and live with you on land for seven years, but at the end of that time you must come with me, and all my goods, and visit my family under the sea. Will you do that, my fine, handsome man?'

'That I will; gladly!'

They fell into each other's arms and their mouths met; the sweetest kisses that Johnny had ever known in his whole life.

The kirk was booked and the minister paid, ready for the big day. It was the talk of the island; Johnny Croy was getting married to some strange lass that no one knew. The folk on Sanday were keen to catch a glimpse of this stranger who had won the heart of their handsome young man. When the day came the mermaid arrived at the kirk wearing a dress of silver and gold. Her long, golden hair hung loose over her shoulders and around her neck was a string of pearls, each one as big as a cockle shell. When the minister prayed she stuffed her hair into her ears, as the mermaids cannot bear to hear the word of God or to see a cross. After they were wed there was a party at Volyar and everyone was amazed by the bride, who danced as light as a feather and whose beauty outshone the local girls.

The mermaid was a good wife. She brewed the strongest and best ale ever tasted in Sanday, was an expert at cooking, baking, spinning and knitting. The house was always as clean and shiny as a new pin; all this as well as the bairns, who came every year. Seven bairns were born at Volyar and each one was beautiful to behold, strong and clever. But the years slipped past and soon the seven years were drawing to an end. The mermaid started to prepare for a journey, putting everything in order and arranging her gear. Her blue cattle that had come with her from the sea were also brushed and made ready to leave. Johnny said nothing, but there was plenty going through his mind. The mermaid sang gently to herself as she made everything ready and in her eyes was a far-away look. Soon everything was in order, apart from the baby boy who was being looked after by Johnny's mother, who lived close by. That night Johnny's mother took a piece of wire, twisted it into the shape of a cross and put it in the fire to heat up. When it glowed red she took the baby on her knee and she branded its backside with the sign of the cross. He roared like a demon!

The day dawned and a boat was seen heading towards the shore below Volyar. In the boat was a crew of fin men; dark, surly characters who seldom spoke. They loaded all of the mermaid's goods into the boat, along with her blue cattle, and then Johnny and the bairns got in the boat too. The only thing left to get was the baby and four fin men were sent to get him. They returned empty handed, saying that they couldn't move the cradle; it was stuck fast to the floor. A dark cloud passed over the mermaid's beautiful face and she ran to the small house where Johnny's mother lived. She ran in, pulled back the blankets of the cradle and tried to pick up her son, but a burning pain shot up both arms and she screamed with pain. She looked at her baby boy lying there and the tears started to fall from her eyes as she slowly turned to go. Granny sat there with tears in her eyes too, but a laugh hung about her mouth. As she left the mermaid lamented, 'Alas, for my bonnie boy. Doomed to live and die among mortals here on land. He will never know that his mother loved him as dearly as she loved her own life.'

With these words the mermaid climbed into the boat and it set sail across the bay and was never seen again by mortal eyes. For Johnny and his mermaid bride never returned to Sanday, but remained in that magical realm under the sea. Their baby boy was known as Corsa Croy, meaning Croy of the Cross, and he grew to be the strongest man in all of Orkney. After his granny died he took to the sword and became a great warrior. He won great fame and fortune for himself as he cut down his enemies like a field of corn falls before the reaper. He amassed a great wealth and married a jarl's daughter in the south country, across the Pentland Firth, and for all I know he might be living yet.

THE CITY UNDER THE SEA

Arthur Dearness was a strong and handsome young man who lived at Corsdale in Sanday, much admired by all the single lasses. But these lasses were to be disappointed because Arthur had fallen in love with Clara Peace, the daughter of the laird of North Skaill, and their marriage had been arranged. However, fame of Arthur's good looks had spread further than his own native island of Sanday and a pair of deep blue eyes watched him from the sea.

One evening, after the harvest had been won and the cold days shortened, Arthur went down to the rocks at Hamaness to gather limpets as bait for his fishing hooks. Arthur had gathered quite a few when he saw a group of fine, big limpets stuck to the face of a rock, just above the sea. He lay flat on his belly to reach over and knock them off with his bait pick. As he lay there he became aware of the sound of music coming from far below him. The sound of the sweet singing grew louder and louder, filling his senses until his

head swam. He had lost the power to move, lying there helpless on the rocks looking down into the sea. Then he saw them, far below, burning bright and as blue as sapphires; a pair of beautiful eyes fixing him with their gaze. A face rose up from the depth of the waters; a face so beautiful that it made Arthur give a little stifled cry of amazement. The next thing that he knew a pair of milk-white arms broke the surface of the water and wrapped themselves around the back of Arthur's neck and drew him lovingly into the sea. What happened next Arthur didn't know, for he had lost all of his senses.

When he woke again he found himself lying in the bow of a little boat that was heading at great speed towards the setting sun with not a sight of land to be seen. In the stern of the boat sat a beautiful mermaid with eyes that shone like sapphires. Her long golden hair hung down to her waist and she wore nothing but a silver-coloured skirt. This skirt was twisted together to form a tail which hung over the stern of the boat and was propelling the boat along. Under this tail-like skirt Arthur could see that the mermaid had a pair of dainty white feet. Then Arthur started to remember his former life, his home, his family and his love, Clara Peace. The mermaid sprang to the front of the boat and kissed Arthur's lips and his memories started to fade. Then she breathed into his mouth; her breath went down his throat like honey and all memories of home left him. In their place was a burning, passionate love for the mermaid and Arthur curled up with her in his arms in the stern of the boat.

The mermaid looked up into the sky until she saw a certain star; Arthur couldn't see it, but mermaids have wonderfully good eyesight. When she saw the star she positioned the boat underneath it and said, in a clear, lyrical voice:

Sea, sea, open to me!
Open the door to Auga

That was the first time that Arthur had heard the mermaid's name; Auga. Suddenly the sea started to churn and to Arthur's horror the boat sank beneath the waves, taking them both with it. Arthur soon became aware that he wasn't drowning; in fact, he could breathe under water like a fish. The boat drifted gently onwards, like a feather on the breeze, going deeper all the time until Arthur saw stretching out beneath him a great city with fine houses made from coral and crystal and studded with precious gems. The boat came gently to rest in the centre of a great square in the middle of the city of Finfolkaheem and Auga took him by the hand and led him to a great palace. As he entered Arthur saw mermaids grinding on a hand-quern. But, instead of grinding corn, they were dropping pearls through the eye of the quern and pearl dust was being scattered onto the floor. Auga took him to a silver room and left him there for a time; staring in wonder at everything that he saw. When she returned she was dressed in a gown of gold and silver and she seemed to radiate beauty as bright as the midday sun. Around her neck was a string of pearls, each one the size of a cockle shell, but she wore no other jewellery, because the brightest diamond would look dull beneath the sparkle of her eyes. They kissed and cuddled for a while before she told him that he must get ready for their wedding. She took a fine robe from a chest and put it on him. Then she called to her servants and two young mermaids took off Arthur's shoes and socks. They washed his feet and anointed them with oils and sprinkled them with pearl dust until they shone.

Arthur was next led into the Foy-Hall, where the wedding celebrations were to take place. The walls, roof and pillars of the Foy-Hall were all made of crystal and it shone with a soft, green phosphorescent glow like you sometimes see on the summer sea. The Foy-Hall was full of fin men and mermaids and they all gave a huge cheer of triumph and welcome as the couple entered. Auga and Arthur were led to the high seats, next to the most important people in the city, and a line of mermaids came and kissed Arthur's feet. Mermaids love the taste of mortal men, but Auga would not allow any of them to kiss him on the lips; they were for her alone. A great feast was set before them of whale, seal and otter meat, every kind of fish, seaweed stewed in seal fat and soup made from whale and seal, thickened with cod roe. Arthur enjoyed this very much and was kept supplied with drinking horns of ale and blood-red wine.

An old fin man with a long white beard tucked into his belt called for silence. He placed a dish with a roast emmer goose[12] in front of them and told them to eat it all between them, pick the bones clean and leave them on the dish as he had to count them when they had finished. As they started to eat Arthur saw that a black cat had appeared on his knee and was starting to pick at some of the meat from Auga's half of the emmer goose. It also took a leg from Arthur's half, picked it clean and put the bone on the plate. It seemed that no one could see the cat but Arthur. When the meat was all finished the old fin man counted the bones and found them to be even. But the cat had broken a powerful spell by taking part of the meat herself. Then they were given a wedding horn, mounted with silver and pearls and filled with the most delicious blood-red wine. Auga drank her half and then handed it to Arthur.

But as Arthur raised it to his lips the cat knocked the bottom of the horn with her head, spilling most of it down between his robe and his skin. Once again the cat knocked into the horn, spilling the wine, but Arthur found that he had no power to prevent the cat from doing this, and so another powerful spell was broken.

Then they all went into the Dancing-Hall, and if the first hall was beautiful than this one was even more wonderful. Along its walls were hung curtains of different coloured lights that shone like the merry dancers[13] on a frosty night. By the fin folk's magic these curtains of light gently shimmered up and down, just like the real ones. The dancing and the drinking went on all night until finally it was time to go to bed. Auga was carried off on a large cushion by two mermaids, while six mermaids danced before her and five behind her. Then two fin men carried Arthur off on a cushion, with six fin men dancing before him and five behind. He was brought into the bedroom where Auga was in bed waiting for him. The fin men undressed him and laid him in the bed next to Auga. Then the thirteen mermaids and the thirteen fin men danced around the bed before leaving them alone. Arthur was very drunk by this time, but he was only human and his desire for Auga was strong. Then he saw the cat again; it was at the foot of the bed and it dived under the blankets and crawled up between them. As it did so it seemed to get longer and thinner until it had turned into an eel, which lay between them. Every time that Arthur tried to touch Auga the eel bit him, but he was so drunk that he soon fell asleep. The last thing that he could remember was the eel whispering sweet nothings in Auga's ear.

The next morning they rose at rising time, as there is no day or night in Finfolkaheem. He went to look around the city and was amazed anew by the beauty of the place. All the fine houses had gardens where lovely coloured seaweeds grew instead of flowers and where brightly coloured fishes darted between their fronds. A huge horn sounded and at that signal the whales and sea cows

were driven towards the city to be milked. Arthur went hunting fish with the fin men, riding on sea horses and using seals and otters like dogs. On his return home Auga would be waiting for him with the finest food, the strongest ale and other unknown pleasures. His days in Finfolkaheem were long and sweet and Arthur never once thought about home or Clara Peace.

Back in Sanday everyone thought that Arthur had been lost. They searched for him and watched the sea in case his body was washed ashore, but he could not be found. Everyone mourned for the loss of Arthur Dearness, but nobody mourned more than young Clara Peace. Her loss was so great that the tears refused to flow; she just sat there, saying nothing, doing nothing but nursing a heart that was broken in two. Her Aunt Marion was sent for, as she had the reputation of being a wise woman. Aunt Marion went to her home at Grindaley and locked herself away in a room. She came out well on through the night and was covered in sweat, like she had been fighting a great battle. She then set off on her horse and rode to Corsdale to see Arthur's parents.

'Your son lives!' she cried. 'And I will bring him back yet. You may well see your son alive again.'

But Arthur's parents just shook their heads in disbelief and said, 'I doubt that. The good wife of Grindaley has got it wrong this time.'

She then rode to North Skaill to see Clara and to tell her the news, but she just sat there, staring into space and said nothing. The light was fading from her eyes.

Back in Finfolkaheem Arthur was sitting with Auga snuggled into his chest. He was holding her with his left arm and stroking her lovely, long golden hair with the other. Suddenly the black cat appeared on his left shoulder, it grabbed his right forefinger between its two paws and it drew a cross on Auga's forehead. She screamed a terrible, loud scream and there was a sound like a clap of thunder. Immediately the light went from Arthur's eyes and he fell to the floor. When he woke up he found himself lying on the rocks at Hamaness with Aunt Marion stooping over him. As he gazed at her in wonder his memory started to return. He remembered his home, his family and Clara Peace. He also remembered the eel and the black cat and, as he looked at Aunt Marion, he seemed to see a familiar look in her eye.

'God bless you and your black cat, Marion, otherwise I would have been bewitched and held in Finfolkaheem for the rest of my life.'

Aunt Marion took him up behind her on her horse and took him straight to Clara. When she saw him the tears that could not flow were released and she held him and sobbed. It was decided that the best thing that they could do was to get married as quickly as possible, and so they did.

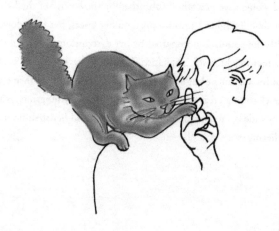

Time has passed and many generations have risen and fallen since the time of Arthur and Clara. But it is said that if you go to the rocks at Hamaness in Sanday as the dawn breaks you can still hear the song of the mermaid Auga drifting on the sea breeze. Only now her song is a lament for a love that is lost and a pain that is hard to bear.

It seems that stories of mermaids were popular as a form of escapism from the harsh realities of poverty, as Walter Traill Dennison wrote in 1892:

> I have seen an old withered woman, with grey hair and wizened face, her head in a sooty cap, a sooty square of homespun over her shoulders, a torn, dirty petticoat of homespun over her knees, her left foot stretched before her on the hearth-stone, that foot in a stocking through which the big toe protruded, her naked right foot stretching over her left, while she was busy darning the stocking she had pulled off for that purpose; while in the midst of her poverty and squalor, she was painting in the most glowing colours, to a group of youngsters, the unequalled charms of the mermaid. The old woman seemed wholly absorbed by the beauty of the being she described; her hands dropped on her knees, her eyes glowed with the enthusiasm imparted by her description; and from the manner in which she emphasised her laudatory words, you could not for a moment but believe that she has seen with her own eyes the charming creature she described, while we youngsters, with eyes wide open and gaping mouths, sat around her spell-bound, believing every word she said.

5

FIN FOLK AND VANISHING ISLANDS

Fin men, although apparently the mermaids' menfolk, were nothing like them. They possessed no tail, but were said to be covered with fins, from which they got their name. They were skilled sorcerers and could wrap these fins around themselves and make them look like items of clothing. They were described as being well-built, black-haired, silent and moody. If you got on the wrong side of a fin man then you were in trouble, as we shall see later.

⟡ THE FIN FOLK AND THE MILL ⟡

At the Bay of Skaill in Sandwick there once stood a fine watermill, although there is nothing left of it now but the millstones and a part of the gears. The sea that uncovered the Neolithic village of Skara Brae next to the mill also ate away at the shoreline, leaving the mill undermined and dangerous. But once it was the scene of a remarkable struggle between the local people of Sandwick and the fin folk that lived nearby, in the waters of the Atlantic Ocean.

The miller at the Mill of Skaill was at his wits' end. Every time he set the millwheel turning to grind the corn that the local crofters had brought to him, his activities were watched by many pairs of greedy eyes. In the bay there lived a number of fin folk and despite the fact that they lived on the produce of the sea they had developed a taste for meal; the flour that the miller ground. As soon as the sun had set the fin folk left their watery realm and crept up to the mill by the shore, as silent as cats, then they burst in through the door, frightened the miller away and stole sacks of flour for their own use. The miller's nerves started to be affected by these nightly raids until he could bear it no longer. He locked up the mill and went home, refusing all pleas from the local folk who wanted him to grind their corn. Time passed and the local crofters found themselves in a very awkward position, as they had to take their corn many miles away to the next nearest mill. Many just didn't bother.

One day an old beggar woman came to the area around the Bay of Skaill and she went from house to house asking if the crofters could spare a bit of flour, or a bannock to allay her hunger. At each door she received the same story; there was no flour to be had since the mill closed. When she asked what had happened she was told about the fin folk and their nocturnal raids on the mill and the miller's fear of returning to his former workplace. The old woman thought for a bit and then said that she could help them, if they would give her everything that she would need. Everyone was eager to get the mill working again and they agreed readily.

'I will need a few things in order to make this plan work,' said the old woman. 'I'll need an iron pot, some fresh water, kale, a ladle, some material for a fire and a spinning wheel with some wool.'

Soon all these things were gathered together and ready to be taken to the mill. The miller refused to go near the place, but he had given them the key to the door. The local folk brought everything to the mill, just as the old woman had asked and then they left in a hurry. Left alone, the old woman lit the fire and hung the pot of water over it to boil before adding the kale and settling down to spin. From the bay the fin folk could see that there was a light burning in the mill and they thought that the miller must have gotten over his fright and returned to work. They left the sea and crept up the beach, over sand and stones, until they reached the door of the mill. With a loud yell they burst through the door and ran from room to room looking for the poor miller and the flour that he had ground, but they saw neither miller nor flour. One fin man went into the room where the old beggar woman sat spinning by her pot of boiling kale. The fin man made horrible sounds and pulled terrible faces to try to frighten her, but she just smiled at him and carried on spinning. The fin man went quiet when he saw that he couldn't frighten the old woman, so he sat down beside her on a creepie[14] and watched her for a while. Knowing that he would gain power over her if she revealed her name to him, he asked her, 'What is your name?'

'Myself in the Mill,' she answered and then she scooped up a ladleful of the boiling water and kale and threw it over the fin man's legs, scalding him badly.

The fin man screamed in pain and ran out of the mill. His cries frightened the others and they all ran out as fast as they could. Once they had calmed down they found their burned friend and asked him, 'Who did this to you?'

'It was Myself in the Mill,' he said.

'Well, if Myself did it then Myself can sail away in the waters with it,' they replied and they went back to the sea and never returned.

The old woman was hailed as a heroine by the local folk, once it became clear that the fin folk had left for good. The miller returned and the crofters could get their corn ground once more. They hung up a straw basket by the door of the mill and everyone who had corn ground there left an offering of flour for the old woman, so she never had to beg again.

∽⊙ THE BLINDING OF TAM SCOTT ⊙∽

Tam Scott was a sailor who ran a large boat from his native island of Sanday. That was until he went blind, of course; so let this story be a warning to you all for I am about to tell you how Tam Scott lost his sight.

It was a sunny day in August and the Lammas Fair was about to begin in Kirkwall. This was a great event with all sorts of folk coming from all over Orkney to sell their goods and have fun. Dealers and merchants, hawkers and showmen came to the fair from as far off as Scotland and Shetland to join in the merriment. It was certainly a sight worth seeing and was eagerly looked forward to by one and all.

Tam Scott and his pal Willie got the boat ready for the voyage from Sanday to Kirkwall. There were plenty of passengers wanting to make use of their vessel and soon they were full and ready to go. Tam smiled a knowing smile to himself as the mothers fussed over their pretty young daughters, for he knew that they would have protected the girls by painting a cross on their breast as a protection in case the fin folk should try to carry them off as their bride. The sign of the cross was a powerful weapon against the fin folk, as was a blessing. The boat sailed swiftly between Eday and Stronsay, past Shapinsay and soon the spire of St Magnus Cathedral was looming large across the bay. Tam and Willie secured the boat, unloaded their passengers and then walked up the narrow, winding street to the Kirk Green in front of the cathedral where the main part of the fair was held. Willie's thirst was bothering him, so he headed to the Anchor Close for a drink. Tam carried on chatting to old friends, catching up with the news and sharing a cog of ale.

After a while a stranger walked over to Tam and said, 'You have a boat for hire, I hear.'

'Yes, I have a boat for hire and a fine boat she is too, in fact …'

'I need you to carry me and a cow to the north isles,' the stranger interrupted. 'I'll make it worth your while for leaving the fair early. I shall meet you at the pier in half an hour.'

Tam went off to find Willie, but there was no sign of him. Eventually he found him lying at the head of the Anchor Close, dead drunk. Tam gave him a kick and cursed his thirst and then headed to the boat to wait for his passenger. Soon he saw the stranger coming down Bridge Street leading a cow. He was a tall man, very well built and with hair and beard as black as a crow. When he got to the boat Tam moved forward to help him get the cow into the boat, but the stranger picked the cow up like it was a sack of wool and set her in the boat. Tam stared in amazement, saying, 'You weren't last in the queue when strength was being dished out.'

The stranger stared at Tam with a frown on his face, but said nothing.

Tam sailed the boat across Kirkwall Bay and headed towards Thieves Holm, where criminals were hanged as a warning to the crews of visiting ships.

'My name's Tam, by the way. I haven't seen you around before. What's your name?'

'A close tongue keeps a safe head,' replied the stranger, glaring at Tam coldly.

'Well, where do you want to go?'

'East of Shapinsay,' said the stranger.

Tam sailed his boat through the String, a stretch of water with powerful currents that can test the best sailors if they are careless. Once the boat was off the east coast of Shapinsay Tam said, 'Where to now then?'

'East of Stronsay.'

Tam was a sociable man and he enjoyed a good chat, but whenever he tried to strike up a conversation the stranger would fix him with a cold stare and say, 'A close tongue keeps a safe head.'

When the boat was off Stronsay Tam asked, 'Do you want to land here?'

'East of Sanday,' came the reply.

'East of Sanday?' said Tam, who was rather confused and getting a little bit annoyed with his passenger.

'What do you mean, east of Sanday? There's nothing east of Sanday but the fjords of Norway and this boat was not built to cross the open sea.'

'East of Sanday,' growled the stranger.

Tam remembered how easily the man had picked up the cow and decided not to argue with him. Instead he turned the boat east past Auskerry and set a course north towards the east coast of Sanday.

As they sailed a fog started to gather around the boat, which caused Tam some concern.

'The fog is drifting in off the North Sea.'

'A close tongue keeps a safe head,' replied the stranger.

'A close tongue might keep a safe head, but a close fog would not be safe for either of us.'

At that the stranger smiled a sulky smile; the first time that Tam had seen him show any sign of mirth. Suddenly the fog lit up like the rays of the rising sun were shining through it and it hung like spun gold on the surface of the sea. The boat sailed into the swirling, dancing mist which blocked out any sight of the islands.

After a short time the fog lifted and there before them Tam saw a beautiful island with fields of ripe corn swaying in the breeze. Men and women were walking around lovely houses and strange blue cattle grazed on the slopes of the green hills; it was the most beautiful sight that Tam would ever see in his life. As the island came into view the stranger leapt to his feet and rushed towards Tam, saying, 'I have to blindfold you now for a time. Do as I say and no harm will befall you.'

Tam remembered the cow being picked up and thought that it would be the safest thing if he went along with the man's demands. He knew now that his passenger must be a fin man and that this was Hilda-Land, their magical floating island home, invisible to mortal eyes. The fin man used Tam's napkin to blindfold him, but it didn't quite cover his eyes and he could see a bit of what was going on. The boat grounded on a gravel beach and Tam heard voices all around him as they unloaded the cow. Then he heard the most beautiful singing as the mermaids began to try to enchant him with their voices, until the fin man shouted, 'You needn't try to cast your spell on him for he has a wife and bairns at home on Sanday.'

When the mermaids heard that their song changed to a sad lament, which was so heartbreaking that the tears came to Tam's eyes. He heard the sound of a bag of money being thrown into the boat and felt the boat pushed off into the sea. The fin man shouted to him, 'Head for starboard and you will soon be home.'

Tam then realised that the fin folk had pushed off the boat against the course of the sun, as they are an unholy race. By the time he removed the blindfold he found himself wrapped up in the fog once more, but soon it cleared and he found himself drifting off the south coast of Sanday in familiar waters.

When Tam got the boat ashore he undid the bag and poured the coins onto the bottom of the boat. He saw that he had been well paid for the journey, but every coin was a copper one. The fin folk love the 'white money' as they call silver, too much to part with it.

A year passed and the Lammas Fair time rolled around once more. Tam was in Kirkwall during the third day of the fair, but many times afterwards he would regret having got out of bed that day. As he was taking a cog of ale he saw the fin man amongst the crowd and he went over to greet him.

'Hello; it's good to see you again. Would you like to join me for a drop of ale? So, what have you been up to since I last saw you?'

'Did you ever see me?' asked the fin man, taking a small box out of his pocket and holding it up to Tam's face.

'You will never have to say that you saw me again.'

With that the fin man blew some of the fine powder that was in the box right into Tam's eyes. Tam screamed as his eyes burned and the sight left them forever. After that time Tam never saw another thing and lived the rest of his days in darkness. So, you see, there is many an evil heart hidden under a fair face, and you should never be too trusting of strangers; especially fin men.

Sometimes, during the summer months, you can see phantom islands floating on the sea where there shouldn't be land at all. These were said to be the summer abodes of the fin folk, called Hilda-Land in the North Isles of Orkney. On Rousay the phantom island was known as Heather Blether and was seen lying out in the Atlantic Ocean, to the west.

I have seen Hilda-Land myself on a couple of occasions; once when I was in a small boat I saw it as a shimmering piece of land between two islands in Scapa Flow. The second time was more unusual and mysterious. It happened in the early 1980s when I was a young man. I was out for a visit to Valdigar, the farm where I was born in Tankerness, and had gone for a walk with two of my elder brothers. When we were on the shore below one of the runways of the airport, looking north, we saw a strange island between Shapinsay and Stronsay. It was quite large and seemed to have a building on it. One of my brothers had a pair of binoculars and so we had the opportunity to study it in some detail. The great grey building was very large and had what looked like a huge arched doorway. None of us could identify the house or the island that it stood on. After about fifteen minutes the island started to slowly melt away, starting at the west end, it shimmered and lifted from the sea. The whole bottom of the island started to slowly vanish, giving it the impression that it was floating over the sea. In the space of about ten minutes it was gone; the middle section with the house being the last to remain. So, what was it? Could it be a part of Sanday brought forward to our sight through refracted light? Or was it really a rare glimpse of Hilda-Land, the home of the fin folk? I shall leave that up to you to decide.

☙ THE VANISHING ISLAND ❧

There was once a fisherman who lived in one of the North Isles with his wife, their two sons and their daughter. Although he also worked the land he had a boat and he and his sons would go out fishing to try to supplement their meagre supply of food, which was often not enough to keep hunger at bay.

One day the man sent his daughter down to the shore to gather limpets for bait for his hooks, but she never returned. They went looking for her and they found her bucket of bait lying on the shore, its contents spilt over the rocks, but there was no sign of the girl. The man had been a fisherman all his life and knew every tide and current that flowed around the island, so if she had fallen into the sea and drowned he knew where her body would come ashore. Every day he searched the rocky headland for his lost daughter, but her body never returned home to them.

The years passed, and the fisherman set off to sea with his sons one fine summer's day. The morning was clear and sunny and the men were in good spirits as they went about the task of setting their lines of hooks in the hope of getting a rich harvest from the sea. Then, to their horror, they saw the fog coming rolling in from the east. They pulled in their lines in the hope of getting their boat near to land before the fog engulfed them, but they were too late. The fog was so thick that they couldn't see a thing in the white-grey gloom that surrounded them. This was a very dangerous situation to be in, because their boat could hit a rock and sink or they could drift out into the ocean and lose sight of land completely. They rowed very slowly around in the hope of seeing land when, to their relief, they saw a dark shape through the murk and they headed towards it. They found themselves approaching an island with a fine gravel beach where they pulled the boat up out of the water, looking around to see if they recognised where they were.

They could see nothing familiar, but they did spot a path leading from the beach. Thinking that a path must go somewhere, they followed it and found that it led to a great big house. This house was much grander than the laird's house back home and they approached it with a nervous feeling. The fisherman knocked on the door and, to his amazement, it was opened by his own daughter; the girl who had gone missing all those years before. There was an emotional reunion and she invited them in. If the outside of the house looked grand then the inside was even more impressive. There were beautiful carpets on the floors, tapestries hanging on the walls, lovely furniture and everywhere there was the glint of silver and gold.

The fisherman asked his daughter how she had come to be there, in such a fine house, when everyone at home had given her up for dead. She said, 'That day, when I went to the shore to gather bait, I forgot what you had always warned me never to do, and I turned my back to the sea. The next thing that I knew a fin man had come out of the sea and grabbed me. I was so scared I forgot to say a blessing on myself, which would have robbed him of his power over me, and he dragged me into his boat. He pulled on the oars and the boat shot across the water like an arrow from a bow, and he took me here to this island, where I have lived ever since. He will be home soon and you'll get to meet him.'

Sure enough, very soon a large, black-haired man came into the house and was introduced to his in-laws by his wife.

'I'm glad to meet you,' he said, in a friendly voice, 'I've heard a lot about you.'

He talked to the fisherman for a while, but no matter how hard the girl's father tried to steer the conversation towards what island they were on the fin man would always change the subject. At last the fin man said, 'Tell me, do you have any cattle to sell?'

'Why, yes,' said the fisherman, 'I do, as it happens. I have a fine cow that I was going to have to send to the market, although I would be sorry to see her go.'

'I'll save you the bother,' said the fin man, 'and I'll pay you well for her.'

He handed the fisherman a bag, and when he looked inside he saw that it was full of gold coins. The fisherman had never seen so much money in his life before. Then it dawned on him that he now had the chance to find out what island they were on.

'Tell me,' said the fisherman, 'what island is this, so that I can bring the cow to you?'

'Never worry about that,' the fin man said, 'I'll come and fetch her myself. But come, there is a meal waiting for us. Eat your fill, and be welcome.'

The table was indeed covered with dishes of fish and seaweed stewed in seal fat; the fin folk have no vegetables, you see. The fisherman and his sons ate their fill, saying that these were the tastiest fish that they had ever eaten, and believe you me, they had eaten plenty of them over the years. Then one of the sons looked out of the window and said, 'The fog's lifting; we can be going soon.'

'Yes, that's right,' said the fin man, 'you can go home soon.'

They started to walk towards the door and were about to say their goodbyes when the girl said, 'Father, is there anything that you would like to take home with you? Any – treasure – which you would like to take with you?'

The fisherman looked at his daughter and smiled.

'Yes, there is a treasure here that I'd like to take home with me.'

'Just name it, and it's yours,' said the fin man.

The fisherman looked at his daughter and smiled, and she smiled back at him.

'You see that big gold dish on the sideboard over there?' he said.

'Take it; it's yours!' said the fin man.

Well, the poor daughter was a bit hurt by this, because, of course, she expected her father to choose her. But I guess he thought that she had a good life there with the fin man and if she came back all that she could expect was hard work, hunger and an early grave. He took the gold dish and the bag of coins and they walked down to the shore where the boat lay. As they were saying goodbye the girl took her father to one side and said, 'Here father, take this token,' and she handed him a knife with a beautiful carved handle. 'As long as you have this knife you will have the power to see this island again and you can come and visit me.'

The fisherman thanked his daughter and turned to help push the boat into the waves.

'Just pull in that direction and you'll be home in no time,' said the fin man.

They pushed the boat into the water and the fisherman jumped in over the stern, but as he did so he dropped the knife into the sea where it sank to the bottom. The fog was all around them again and the island was lost from view. Suddenly, they came out of the fog bank and found themselves back in bright sunshine again, and to their astonishment, they were in the bay right below their own home. They sailed to the shore and pulled the boat up into the noust[15] and headed home. They were met by the fisherman's wife, who came hurrying to meet them.

'Oh, thank god you are safe,' she said, 'I was worried sick when I saw that fog coming in.'

'Oh, we're fine,' said the fisherman.

'Well, I'll tell you something that's not fine,' said his wife, 'Brenda, our best cow, is gone!'

'Gone?' said the fisherman. 'What do you mean, gone?'

'Gone as in gone,' snorted his wife, 'how many "gones" are there? I went into the byre just now and she's gone.'

The fisherman smiled to himself. He knew that the fin man had used his magic to transport the cow to their island.

'Never you worry about her,' he said to his wife, 'she was well paid for.'

He showed his wife the bag of gold coins and told her the story of their daughter and the fin man. He showed her the dish too and she was amazed by it all. After that the fisherman was rich, and if he had to go out fishing again it was because he liked to fish and not because he had to. But he had lost that knife and so, no matter how often or how hard he tried he never saw that island again and he never saw his daughter again either. So I'm not so sure that he was that rich after all.

The fog that swept in around the fisherman's boat is an all-too-dangerous occurrence in the summer months in Orkney. The warm waters of the Gulf Stream, which keeps the temperature above freezing in the winter months, meets the cold waters from the North Sea and, mixed with warm air from the land on a hot summer's day, turns to fog. You can watch it rolling in over the sea at an alarming speed. My mother, Lizzie Drever, was born in the small croft of North Tuan in Westray in 1922. When she was a little girl she would be sent off to the headland called the Point of Sponess when the fog came in and her father was at sea in his boat, the *Spray*. He would be setting creels to catch lobsters to sell and crabs to eat; nobody at that time would ever dream of buying a partan, as the large edible crabs are called in Orkney. They were considered a pest in those days, not a delicacy, but were eaten or given away to old people in the community. When my grandfather was in trouble, lost in the fog, my mother would go to that headland and look for a small seashell that she called a 'whistling buckie', known in English as a flat periwinkle. These small shells come in various colours, green, brown, orange, yellow, and in banded and striped varieties. If you angle them just right and blow into them then they can produce a loud, high-pitched whistle (although this only works with the larger ones). My mother would stand there and blow into her shell and her father would hear her and, putting his fingers into his mouth, he would whistle back in reply. She would slowly walk along the shore, whistling as she went and listening for the reply until she reached the boat noust where the boat was secured. These were cut into the banks of the seashore, sometimes lined with stone, as a shelter for the boat. This practice dates back to at least Viking times, as the archaeological record shows. Once at the noust she would stand and whistle until she saw her father's boat coming through the fog; the youngest child bringing her father safely home from the sea.

⊙ Eynhallow ⊙

The lovely little island of Eynhallow lies between the West Mainland parish of Evie and the island of Rousay. It was called Eyn Helga (Holy Island) by the Vikings and has a well-preserved twelfth-century chapel with monastic buildings around it. It is thought to be the place where the powerful chieftain Sven Asleifarson sent his son to be educated. Where it lies two tides meet and there is often broken water, churning white with foam, raging on either side of it, which is called a 'roost' in Orkney (Old Norse *röst*; a tidal stream). This is recorded in an old children's rhyme:

> Eyn-Hallow frank, Eyn-Hallow free,
> Eyn-Hallow lies in the middle of the sea,
> Wae a roaring roost on either side,
> Eyn-Hallow lies in the middle of the tide.

But Eynhallow was not always there, as we shall see.

The goodman of Thorodale was married and had three grown-up sons by his wife. But one day she took ill and soon died; much to the sorrow of her husband and children. After a period of mourning Thorodale started to think that he might look for another wife, as he wasn't that old and was still strong and handsome to look at. His attention turned to a young woman who was said to be the most beautiful girl in all of Evie. He wooed her and she agreed to marry him and came to live with him at his home. She got on well with his sons and everything was going fine for Thorodale, until one fateful day when he and his wife went to the shore to gather shellfish. Thorodale had just sat down on a rock to tie his rivlin[16] when he heard his wife scream. As he turned around he saw a fin man carrying her into a boat and pulling on the oars. The boat took off at fantastic speed and was lost from sight before Thorodale could do anything. He cried out in rage and heartbreak and, going down on his knees below the high water mark, he swore an oath that he would get his revenge on the fin folk somehow.

Time passed and one day, as Thorodale was out fishing between Evie and Rousay, he heard the sound of a woman's voice singing. He recognised it as the voice of his lost wife, although he couldn't see her. As he listened he realised that she was singing to him; she sang:

Goodman, greet[17] no more for me,
For me again you'll never see;
If you would have of vengeance joy,
Go speer[18] the wise spaewife[19] of Hoy.

Thorodale headed to the shore, put his silver in his sock and walked out to the shores of Scapa Flow from where he took a boat to Hoy. Here he met the spaewife who told him that there was nothing that he could do to get his wife back, but what would hurt the fin folk more than anything else was to lose any part of Hilda-Land. She told him what he had to do and he set off for home again. Every night when the moon was full he would go to the Odin Stone in Stenness. This stone is sadly no longer there, but it was an outlier of the Stones of Stenness and had a hole through it. It had an uncanny reputation; it could cure ills and if you held hands through it and made the Odin Oath then you were as good as married. So, for nine nights on the night of the full moon, Thorodale would go on his bare knees nine times around the stone and then look through the hole in it. On the final night he was shown what he must do. He went home and got a meal girnal[20] and filled it full of salt and then set three caisies[21] on top of it. He told his three sons what they had to do when the time came and then he waited.

One fine summer's morning Thorodale got up and went outside. He yawned, stretched and looked out over the sound towards Rousay, and there he saw it; a beautiful green island where there had never been one before. He kept his eyes fixed on the island and shouted to his sons to get things ready. They carried the girnal of salt down to the boat, and a heavy lift that was for them. They took the caisies on their backs too and they put everything into the stern of the boat. They pushed the boat down to the water and Thorodale leapt into the bow of the boat, never taking his eyes off

that island. His sons couldn't see it; no one could, only Thorodale, and if he took his eyes off it for just a moment he would never see it again.

As the three boys rowed the boat Thorodale stood in the bow, staring at the island. Suddenly, a school of whales came swimming in through the sound. The boys got excited, shouting that they should try to herd the whales ashore for their oil, which would bring them a good price. Thorodale shouted in a gruff voice, 'Carry on rowing; you will get no oil from them, boys.'

Then the largest whale broke away from the rest and swam towards the boat; its huge mouth open as if it would swallow them whole. The boys were frightened, but Thorodale took a handful of salt and threw it into the monster's gaping mouth and it disappeared from sight. Thorodale knew that the fin folk were using their magic to conjure up phantoms in order to frighten them and to distract them from their task in hand. Then, as the boat got nearer to the shore, the mermaids started to sing. Their voices were so beautiful that the boys' heads started to swim. They started to row slower and slower, but Thorodale kicked the ones nearest to him and shouted, 'Row, damn you!'

Then he took a cross that he had made by twisting together dried tangles[22] and threw it at the mermaids, saying, 'Take that, you unholy limmers!'[23]

On seeing the sign of the cross the mermaids screamed and dived into the sea with a splash.

Then the boat grounded on a gravel shore; this was the first time that the boys could see that there was an island. Thorodale jumped out onto the shore, only to be faced with a huge monster. It had feet as big as millstones, tusks as long as a man's arm and it spat flames from its mouth. Thorodale took a handful of salt and threw it into the monster's face; it disappeared with an awful growl. There, in its place, stood a fin man with a drawn sword. Thorodale recognised him as the same fin man who had carried

off his wife. The fin man spoke, saying, 'Go back from where you came. I know why you've come here; you've come to steal part of Hilda-Land. But I'm warning you; leave now or by my father's head I'll defile this land with your vile, human blood.'

The boys in the boat were afraid and shouted to their father, 'Quick, run! Come back to the boat!'

But Thorodale stood his ground. The fin man lunged at Thorodale, slashing his sword through the air, but Thorodale jumped to one side and threw another cross at the fin man. This one was made of a kind of sticky grass called 'cloggers', which stuck to the fin man's face. He screamed in pain as the sign of the cross burned his skin, but he dare not touch it in order to pull it off as this would burn his hands. He turned around and ran away, roaring in agony.

'Be quick boys,' shouted Thorodale, 'you know what to do.'

His three sons got out of the boat, taking the girnal of salt and the caisies with them. They filled the caisies full of salt and went around the island, three abreast, sowing salt in a ring around the edge of the island. Three times they went around the island sowing nine rings of salt right around Eynhallow. Thorodale cut nine crosses into the turf to sanctify it and to fix it in place for good. The fin folk roared in anger, the mermaids screamed, their lovely blue cattle bellowed and they all ran down the slopes and into the sea. And that is how the fin folk lost Eynhallow. But, the youngest boy had big hands and he ran out of salt before he could finish his last ring of salt. He asked his brothers if they could spare him some, but they said that they only had enough to finish their rings, so the ninth ring of salt was never completed. That is why it is said that Eynhallow is still a magical place. No rats, cats or mice can live there, iron stakes used to tether animals jump out of the ground after sunset and if you try to cut crops after sunset the stalks bleed. It is said that stones from Eynhallow were used in Kirkwall houses to keep away vermin by burying them under the threshold of the door. Soil from Eynhallow was carted to Westness in Rousay to spread over the stackyard to keep rats and mice out of the corn stacks. If you are lucky enough to visit the island you will experience a strange feeling of a magical and ancient place; somehow outside of time.

6

SELKIE FOLK

In Orkney seals are called selkies, but they are not always what they seem. There are two kinds of selkies that usually live in Orkney; the common or harbour seal likes sheltered water while the larger Atlantic grey seal can be found in more exposed coastal areas. The grey seal is the most common species in Orkney, which is a major breeding area for them. It was these larger seals that were true selkies, and they contain a secret inside. It was said that people who had drowned were turned into seals, but at certain times of the tide they could remove their skin, taking human form for one night and on that night they danced together.

On a visit to my family sometime in the early 1980s I decided to stay overnight. I sat up late (as usual) reading a book far into the night. As the night wore on I became aware of a strange sound coming from outside; it was the sound of a woman sobbing. I listened closely, and the sobbing continued. It was coming from the direction of the shore below our farm, quite a few hundred yards away. The sobbing was heartbreaking and I found myself deeply moved and troubled by the sound. What was going on? There was an old road that ran by the shore; the former road from Tankerness to Kirkwall before the wartime aerodrome was built. Had there been an accident? Was someone hurt and needing attention? The sobbing continued, but then it broke away in an unearthly groan that was not human. The blood in my veins ran cold. After a short time the sobbing began again, followed by the groan. This was definitely not human, but what was it? Then it dawned on me; it was the sound of a selkie by the shore. They make a strange array of sounds, from haunting high-pitched calls to grunts and growls, but they also, on rare occasions, sob. Maybe this was the reason behind the story of selkie women being taken as a wife?

THE SELKIE OF WESTNESS

The goodman of Westness in North Ronaldsay had a mistrust of women and said that he would never be foolish enough to marry. The local girls looked at him with distaste, saying that he was a very old young man. One old woman was deeply offended by his remarks and said that maybe he would find himself bewitched by a woman's charms, but he just laughed and said that it was unlikely to happen. However, fate had other plans for him, as we will see.

One fine summer's day the man of Westness was walking along the shore when he heard the sound of laughter. This seemed strange to him and he wondered who it could be. He saw, in the distance, that there were a lot of beautiful young people playing by the rocky shore while on the other side of a shallow pool lay a pile of seal skins. He knew that this was the selkie folk who had left the sea and taken off their skins and so he crept along the shore, unseen by the selkies, until he was near the pile of skins. Once there he started to run as fast as he could towards the skins, but the selkie folk had seen him and they ran towards them too. One after the other they snatched up their skins and fled back to the sea. But the man of Westness was quick and he was able to grab one of the very last skins. He turned around and walked back towards his home but behind him he could hear the sound of footsteps on the shore and the sound of a woman sobbing quietly to herself. Turning back he saw a sight that made his heart skip a beat, for there stood a beautiful young selkie woman. She had long dark hair, big brown eyes and was as naked as the day that she was born. With the salt tears trickling down her cheeks she begged him, 'Please give me back my skin. I can't go back to my home in the sea without it. I can't see my family again, or my loving man, if I don't have my skin. If you ever hope to have pity yourself one day, then please have pity on me and give me back my skin.'

The man of Westness looked at her, and the more that he looked at her the more he desired her. He wanted her, he craved her; he must possess her.

'No,' he said, 'I won't give you back your skin. You will come with me to my home and you will be my wife.'

Her pleas were wasted on him. The man of Westness had set his heart on her and no matter how many tears she shed he would not set her free. The selkie had no choice but to follow him home and be his wife. They were soon married and had seven children, four boys and three girls. It was said that there had never been such bonnie bairns born in North Ronaldsay before. But the selkie woman was sad all her time on land and she never stopped searching for her stolen skin. Sometimes she would slip away by herself and sit and stare out to sea. Sometimes a big bull seal would rise up from the sea and swim back and fore, staring at her as she wept bitter tears.

The years passed and the boys were old enough to go out to the fishing with their father. On one such occasion the selkie woman was left in the house with their youngest girl, who had cut her foot and the wound had become infected. The child sat on a chair with her sore foot on a stool while her mother pretended to clean the house. She was, of course, looking for her seal skin.

'What are you looking for mother?' asked the little girl.

'Oh, don't tell anyone, but I'm looking for a bonnie skin to make you a pair of rivlins to help heal your sore foot.'

The little girl smiled and said, 'I know where there's a bonnie skin hidden.'

The selkie woman froze, and turned to her child, 'Where did you see it?'

'One day,' said the little girl, 'when I was lying in the bed and Dad thought that I was sleeping he took a bonnie skin down from the top of the wall above the bed and he looked at it for a while and then he set it back again.'

The selkie woman ran to the spot and ran her hand along the top of the wall, where the rafters sat on top of it, and her hand touched something familiar. She pulled it out and there was her skin. She turned to her child and said, 'Farewell to you, my peedie[24] buddo,'[25] and with that she ran out the door and down to the shore. She pulled on her seal skin and dived into the water. A big bull seal swam over to her and there was a happy reunion between them. Just at that moment the man of Westness rounded the headland in his boat. The selkie woman swam over to it and, raising the skin from her face sang this rhyme:

> Good man of Westness,
> Farewell to thee!
> I liked you well,
> You were good to me.
> But I loved better my man of the sea.

With that she pulled the skin back over her face and dived under the sea. The man of Westness and his seven children never saw her again.

❦

Not all selkie wives were so keen to return to the sea, as we will see in this next tragic story.

❦ The Selkie Wife ❧

There was once a young man in the East Mainland parish of Deerness who was going home late one night. What he was doing out so late I have no idea, but he was walking along the shore on his way home. He thought that he could hear something drifting towards him on the breeze; it was the sound of music. On along the shore he walked and he could hear the music getting louder and louder as he went. He slowed his pace down, treading carefully and quietly along until he found a piece of rock jutting out and he hid behind it. Peeping around the rock he saw that the music was coming from two men sitting on a flat rock and playing fiddles. There, on a sandy piece of the shore in front of them, was a crowd of people all dancing in a great circle. The moonlight shone on their white skin as they danced round and round, laughing with delight. All around them the man could see the shape of animals lying asleep. He very carefully crawled along the beach towards the sleeping animals, to see what they were. When he got there he saw that they were not animals at all, but seal skins; empty seal skins. He knew then that these were selkie folk and that this must be their night to dance.

One of the skins was lovelier than the rest; it was silvery coloured and silky smooth to the touch. He rolled it up and put it under his jacket and then returned to his hiding place to watch them dance. But as soon as the first light of dawn peeped over the horizon the music stopped and they all ran to their skins, pulled them on and slipped back into the sea. All, that is, except for one young girl who frantically searched among the rocks and seaweed for her missing skin. In her panic she ran right around the corner of the rock where the man was hiding; right into his arms. He clutched her tight and looked into her large, beautiful eyes and he thought that she was the most beautiful girl that he had ever seen and that he would never be happy until he had her for his wife. She, on the other hand, had other ideas! She punched him, kicked him and scratched him, skreeking[26] out of her in the selkie tongue, for the selkies have their own way of speaking. But he was too big and strong for her and he carried her off to his home where he lived with his mother.

Now, what he said when he came home with a naked girl under one arm and a seal skin under the other, I don't know. But his mother was a kind-hearted soul and she took great care of the selkie girl. The poor girl just sat by the fire, sobbing her heart out, for days on end. But eventually she calmed down and the old woman got her used to wearing clothes and taught her how to speak. She also taught her how to cook and bake and brew ale, spin wool and knit and do all the things that it was thought necessary for a woman to do in those days. After a while it became obvious that the selkie girl liked the young man too, for she always followed him around and was always happy in his company. It was no surprise when they were married and set up home together. In fact it was said that there was not a more beautiful bride seen in Deerness than the selkie girl. After a while they had bairns and they were also very beautiful and clever children. The man took the seal skin and locked it up, safe and sound, in the big kist[27] in the ben end[28] of the house.

One day the selkie wife took her husband to one side and said to him, 'You know that I am a creature of the sea, and I know that you have my skin and I know where you keep it; it's in the big kist in the ben end of the house. I also know that you keep the key on you at all times. But I want you to make me a promise. I'm happy here, with you and the bairns, but if I ever get my hands on that skin then I can't promise that I could resist the urge to go back to the sea. So, if you love me, if you really love me, then never let me get hold of that skin. Do you promise?'

'Yes, I promise,' he said.

Now, it was one August and the Lammas Fair was in full swing in Kirkwall. This was a great market where you could buy

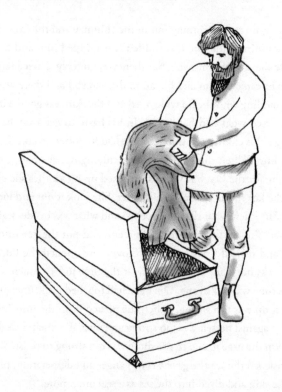

everything from a hen's leg to a horse. People came from all over Orkney and from Shetland and the north of Scotland as well. They arrived in their numbers to buy and sell, and there were games and fun things to do for the bairns too. It was a great occasion, and the man thought that it would be a great treat to take his bairns to see it. He got a horse and cart ready to go and, once the bairns were washed and dressed in their Sunday best, he put on his best clothes as well and they set off for the town. The selkie woman didn't go with them though; she decided to stay and give the house a thorough clean while they were away.

That evening, as the man turned the cart for home, the bairns were curled up asleep in the back. But when he got near the house he could see that something was wrong. There was no light in the window, no smoke coming out of the chimney and the front door was standing wide open. A sudden fear gripped him and he ran inside shouting for his wife, but there was no reply. Then a terrible thought came to him and he ran to the ben end and there was the kist standing with the lid wide open and the skin was gone. Finally he realised what had happened. In his haste to get away he had changed his clothes in a hurry and he had forgotten to take the key with him. When the selkie wife was tidying up, she hadn't been looking for the key, but when she picked up his clothes she could feel the key in the pocket of his jacket. She took it out and looked at it. She knew what that key opened and what was inside, waiting for her. She ran through to the ben end and put the key into the lock and turned it with a click. Slowly she opened the lid, and there was her skin. When she saw it the urge just to touch it one more time was too strong. Once she had touched it the urge just to pick it up was too strong. When she picked it up the urge just to hold it against herself was too strong and once she smelt the salt on the skin the urge to run to the shore was too strong to resist. When she reached the sea she gave a cry of anger and desperation, pulled on the skin and dived into the sea as a seal once more.

The man searched along the shore for his selkie wife, but he never saw her again for as long as he lived. But it was said that when the bairns used to go down to the shore to play, a selkie would swim backwards and forwards in front of them; sobbing like its heart was breaking.

It was not just selkie women who had relationships with humans, sometimes selkie men would quite willingly seek out a human lover, as the following story demonstrates.

∞ URSILLA AND HER SELKIE LOVER ∞

Ursilla Balfour was the daughter of the laird of Stronsay, his only child and heir to his estate. She was a beautiful young woman, but she was proud, overbearing, strong willed and quick to anger. Her father tried to push her into marriage; not for love but as a good financial business transaction. If she married the son of another laird then it would unite two wealthy families and increase their fortune and reputation. But Ursilla was having none of it. No matter how hard her father tried she would always send away the hapless suitors who came to court her. It looked like Ursilla would never marry, but there was a very good reason why she refused to accept the proposals that she received. You see, Ursilla Balfour was already in love. The object of her desires was not the son of a rich laird, but the man who worked in her father's barn. She watched him go about his work and the fires of love burned fiercely inside her. But she had to hide her feelings and she did this very well for she treated the poor man like dirt. He was often on the wrong end of Ursilla's sharp tongue and many a row he received from her. However, as long as her father lived, Ursilla had to keep her love for the barn man a secret.

One day Ursilla's luck changed and her father died, leaving her with all his land and money. The first thing that she did was to go to the barn man and say, 'Right you; get home and wash and shave.'

'Why?' he asked, somewhat puzzled by her order.

'Because you're going to be married.'

'Married,' he spluttered, 'married to whom?'

'Why, married to me of course! Don't you know that I love you?'

'Eh, no,' he said, even more confused than before, 'I can't say that I had noticed.'

'Well, I do, and you need a wash and a shave before I get you ready for our marriage. Hurry up now; run along!'

∞

The poor man was in a terrible fix. He certainly didn't love her, in fact, he didn't even like her. But she was the laird now and her word was law. If he refused he would be evicted from his house and would have to find himself a new home on another island. Maybe Ursilla would take out her anger on his family and his parents, brothers and sisters might suffer the same fate. No, he had to do it, no matter how much the idea appalled him. Ursilla, meanwhile, wasted no time in sending out the wedding invites to all the lairds whose sons had failed to win her. It caused quite a scandal; Ursilla Balfour marrying a common farm servant. How awful!

'It won't last,' they said, 'six months; that's all I give it. Marrying so far beneath yourself; it's disgusting!'

But Ursilla didn't care, she loved her handsome barn man and she was going to marry him no matter what they said. But the old saying is true; 'marry in haste, repent at leisure', and that's what happened to Ursilla Balfour. The man didn't love her and the marriage bed remained a cold, lonely place. She soon came to realise that she had acted too rashly in marrying the man. But it was too late to do anything about it and she didn't want to give the other lairds the satisfaction of saying, 'I told you so!'

She had to maintain the pretence of a happy marriage, but she was a passionate woman and she had needs. If her husband didn't love her then she would take a lover to keep her warm at night. But if she was found out then there would be another scandal and she couldn't trust any of the lairds' sons to keep quiet about such an arrangement. However, Ursilla was a strong-willed, determined woman and she decided that she would find a lover among the selkie folk. She went down to the sea early one morning and waited until the tide was full and then she shed seven tears into the water. Some folk said that they were the only tears that she ever shed in her life. As the ripples from the final tear were fading away the head of a great selkie broke the surface of the water and swam towards her. When it was near it rose from the water and pulled back the skin, revealing a strong, handsome face.

'What do you want from me, fair lady?' asked the selkie man.

'I have made a bad marriage and the bed is a cold, unloving place. I want to feel strong arms around me. I want to be loved and to make love.'

'So, you've come to the selkie folk?'

'Yes, I have.'

'Well, I will come to you and satisfy your needs, but I can only take human form every seventh stream.[29] Meet me here at that time.'

With that the selkie man covered his face and slid beneath the waves.

At the next seventh stream Ursilla hurried to the shore and the selkie man rose up and shed his skin and they embraced. All of Ursilla's needs and desires were answered that night and when it was time for them to part she promised to come back to him at the next seventh stream.

It was noted that Ursilla was in a much better mood after that. Her servants also noticed that she was putting on weight, especially around the belly. As the time passed it became obvious that there was more than one heart beating inside Ursilla's body. When her time came she gave birth to a fine baby boy, strong limbed, brown eyed and with webbed hands and feet. Now didn't that tell a story? The nurse clipped the webs of skin between the fingers and toes, but they kept growing back again. The nurse continued to clip them until, as they couldn't grow in the usual place, they spread onto the palms of the hands and the soles of the feet as a horny, thick skin. It is said that this condition, known as 'hard hands' in Stronsay, is still to be seen in the descendant of Ursilla Balfour and her selkie lover to this day.

7

TWO CLASSICS AND A TRAVELLERS' TALE

These next two tales are classic stories that were said to be collected by Andrew Lang (1844–1912) from an old woman in Rousay in the late nineteenth century and published in *Longman's Magazine* in 1889. Lang is famous for his series of 'Rainbow Fairy Books' that were published from 1889–1910, but he was not an active collector so the claim may be false. These two stories were hailed as a true representation of old folk tales that had not been interfered with. They have elements of European tales and from the description of the wooded countryside in 'Kate Crackernuts' it could not have been inspired by the treeless landscape of Orkney and is more akin to the tales of the Scottish Travellers. 'Peerie Fool' also has elements of well-known European and Scandinavian folk tales, although the old woman told the Orkney folklorist Duncan J. Robertson that this was an old Orkney story. The word 'peerie' means 'little' and is still used in Shetland. The earliest Orkney dialect writing uses the word 'peerie', but in Orkney it changed into 'peedie' during the nineteenth century.

ເ⊛ Kate Crackernuts ⊛ວ

There was once a king who had a beautiful young daughter called Anne who was the apple of his eye. However, tragedy struck the family when Anne's mother, the queen, took ill and died. After a while the king married again, taking a widowed queen as his wife. This queen had a daughter called Kate, who was about the same age as Anne. Kate loved nothing more than cracking nuts and eating them, so she was called Kate Crackernuts. Although these two princesses were not related they loved each other like true sisters. The queen, on the other hand, was jealous of Anne as she was more beautiful than her own daughter and she decided that she would find a way to spoil her lovely looks. She paid a visit to the hen wife who lived in a little tumbled-down cottage in the woods and kept the castle supplied with eggs. The hen wife was a black-hearted witch and she plotted with the queen to curse young Anne and rob her of her beauty.

'Send her to me tomorrow morning first thing,' said the hen wife, 'and make sure that she is fasting.'

The next morning the queen got Anne up early and told her to go to the hen wife to collect eggs. She got up, dressed, took a basket and went down the back stairs. As she was passing the kitchen she saw a piece of bread and so she took it and ate it on the road. When she reached the hen wife's cottage she knocked at the door and heard a voice telling her to come in. She opened the door and saw in the inky blackness inside that there was a pot boiling over a fire.

'Lift the lid of the pot and see,' said the hen wife.

Anne lifted the lid of the pot but saw nothing other than a broth bubbling away. The hen wife seemed annoyed, telling her, 'Go home and tell your mother to keep the larder door bolted.'

The queen was angry when she heard this, as she knew that the princess must have eaten something, but she said nothing. The next day she sent Anne back to the hen wife, but this time she went to the door with her, to make sure that she didn't have anything to eat on the way. As Anne walked down the road she met some people who were picking peas and they gave her some to eat. When she lifted the lid of the pot for a second time nothing happened.

'Tell your mother that the pot can't boil without the fire,' said the hen wife.

The queen was very angry this time, as she knew that the girl must have eaten something, so on the third morning she went with her all the way to the hen wife's cottage, just to make sure. This time when Anne was told to lift the lid of the pot she again saw the broth bubbling away but suddenly a sheep's head popped up to the surface and stared at her. Then Anne's beautiful head fell off and the sheep's head jumped onto her shoulders and took its place. The queen and the hen wife laughed at her, but she could do nothing but weep. When the queen took her back to the castle and Kate saw her they both cried on each other's shoulder. Then Kate carefully wrapped up Anne's head in bandages and led her out of the castle. They walked and walked a long way, searching for a cure for Anne's condition and to escape the evil queen.

After a while they came to another kingdom and headed towards the castle. Kate knocked on the door and said that she had travelled a very long way and that her sister was ill. Since they were both very tired and hungry she asked if they had any work that she could do in return for a bed and something to eat. Soon she was given a job in the kitchen washing pots and peeling vegetables. However, Kate noticed that the castle was not a happy place, everyone seemed sad and there was no music or laughter. She was told that the king's eldest son was gravely ill and near to death. He was growing weaker every day by some sort of sorcery, but no one was brave enough to sit with him all night to find out the cause of it. Kate said that she would sit with him that night if she was paid a peck of silver and the king was happy to agree to this.

That night Kate was sat by the fireside cracking nuts when the clock struck midnight. Suddenly the prince's eyes opened and he got up and dressed. Then he slipped down the back stairs, followed by Kate, and headed to the stable where he saddled his horse, called for his hound and rode away into the night. Kate jumped up behind him; the prince never even noticed that she was there. As they rode through the woods Kate plucked nuts from the trees and put them into the pocket of her apron. Eventually they reached a large, green hill and the prince called out, 'Open! Open, green hill, and let the young prince in with his horse and his hound.'

'And his lady behind him,' said Kate.

The green hill opened and they rode inside. There was a beautiful hall within the hill, brightly lit and richly furnished. The prince got off the horse and was surrounded by beautiful fairy ladies who led him away to dance while Kate hid behind the door and watched. They danced with him all night long and if he swooned on a sofa they would fan him and then raise him up to dance again. This was what was wrong with him; he was being danced to death by the fairies. When the cock crowed the prince mounted his horse and Kate jumped up behind him and they rode back to the castle where he went back to his bed. Kate sat once more by the fire, cracking nuts and eating them.

The next morning the king was delighted to find her there. She said that he had passed a peaceful night. She was offered a peck of gold to sit with him for another night and she willingly accepted. Again she sat with the prince and it all went the same that night as it had done on the first night. The prince rose, saddled his horse and rode to the green hill to dance with the fairy ladies all night long. This time Kate hid behind the door and saw a small fairy child playing with a wand. She overheard one of the fairies say to another, 'If only Kate knew that three strokes of that wand would make her sister as beautiful as ever.'

Kate rolled nuts towards the fairy child and he dropped the wand and chased after them. Kate took the wand, slipped it into her apron pocket and left with the prince when the cock crowed.

The following morning the king was delighted to see Kate still sitting with his son. He asked her what price she would take to stay a third night with him. Kate asked to marry him, and so it was agreed. Kate then rushed off to the room where her sister was and gave her three strokes on the head with the wand. The sheep's head tumbled off and her own beautiful head jumped onto her shoulders just like she was before.

That night went the same as the first two, with the prince riding to the green hill and dancing with the fairy ladies. Kate hid behind the door and saw the fairy child was playing with a brightly coloured bird. She overheard one of the fairies say to another, 'If only Kate knew that three bites of that bird would cure the sick prince.'

She rolled nuts over the floor towards the child who dropped the bird and ran after them. Kate grabbed the bird, put it in her apron pocket and left with the prince when the cock crowed.

That night, instead of sitting cracking nuts by the fireside, Kate plucked the bird and started to roast it over the fire. Soon a delicious aroma filled the room and the prince opened his eyes and said, 'Oh, if only I had a bite of that bird.'

Kate gave him a bite and the prince raised himself up on one elbow and said, 'Oh, if only I had another bite of that bird.'

Kate gave him a second bite and the prince sat up and said, 'Oh, if only I had a third bite of that bird.'

Kate gave him a third bite and the spell was broken. When the king came into the room the following morning he saw Kate and the prince sitting by the fire, cracking nuts together. He was delighted and the wedding was arranged. The prince had a brother and when he saw Anne, looking so beautiful again, he fell in love with her and they were married too. So the sick prince married the well sister and the well prince married the sick sister and they lived there in peace and happiness for the rest of their days and never drank out of a dry cup.

PEERIE FOOL

There was once a king and queen who lived in Rousay with their three daughters. The king died and the queen and the princesses fell on hard times until all they had left was a small house, a cow and a kale yard. It started to become obvious that someone was stealing their kale during the night, so the eldest princess decided that she would wrap a blanket around herself and sit out all night to watch for the thief. Nothing happened until the very middle of the night. Then the princess saw a huge giant come striding over the kale yard wall, dump a big straw basket on the ground and start to cut the kale. She shouted at him to stop, asking him why he was taking her mother's kale, but he just looked at her and said, 'If you are not quiet I will take you too.'

Once the giant had filled his basket he grabbed the princess by the arm and leg, tossed her into the basket on top of the kale and carried her off.

When they got to the giant's house he told her that she had to work for him. He wanted her to milk the cow and put it out to pasture on the high hill. Then she had to wash, comb, card, spin and weave a great pile of wool. If the cloth was not ready when he came home then she would be in trouble. The eldest princess milked the cow and put it out to the pasture on the high hill and then came back to the giant's house. She was hungry and so she took a pot and started to make some porridge for her breakfast. Then, all of a sudden, a whole lot of tiny yellow-haired people came crowding around her, begging for a bite to eat, but the princess refused, saying:

Little for one and less for two,
And never a grain have I for you.

When she tried to work the wool she found that nothing would go right and so when the giant returned that night he found the wool still lying where it was. He took the princess and tore a strip of skin from the crown of her head, down her back and over her heels and he threw her over the rafters with the hens. She could neither move nor speak.

The next night the middle princess wrapped a blanket around herself and sat out in the kale yard to see who was stealing the kale and who had taken her sister. The giant arrived and started to cut the kale. The princess scolded him but he picked her up by the arm and the leg, tossed her in the basket and took her home. Everything happened the same as with the eldest sister, she milked

the cow and put it out to the pasture on the high hill and then put
on the pot to make porridge. The tiny yellow-haired people came
crowding around and asked for a bite to eat, but the princess said:

> Little for one and less for two,
> And never a grain have I for you.

If the wool didn't work for her sister it went even worse for her.
The giant came home and found the wool untouched and he tore
a strip of skin from the crown of her head, down her back and over
her heels. Then he threw her over the rafters alongside her sister
and the hens.

On the third night the youngest princess sat out in the kale
yard, wrapped in a blanket. The giant came and started to cut the
kale and the princess begged him to leave the little food that they

had, but he just snorted and said that if she wasn't quiet he'd take
her too. When he had filled his basket he grabbed her by the arm
and leg, threw her on top of the kale and carried her off to his
home. He gave her the same orders as her sisters; to milk the cow
and put her out to the pasture on the high hill and then to take the
big pile of wool and wash it, comb it, card it, spin it and weave it
into cloth. All of this had to be done before he returned. So the
youngest princess milked the cow and put her out to the pasture
on the high hill and then she put on the pot to make porridge for
her breakfast. Suddenly the room was full of tiny little people with
yellow hair all begging for a bite to eat. The youngest princess was
very kind and soft-hearted, so she said, 'Find yourself something to
sup with and you can share my porridge.'

They all ran out and then returned with spoons made from
heather stems and pieces of broken dishes and they all supped the
porridge with her until it was all gone. They all left, except for one
tiny little boy with yellow hair, who said, 'Do you have any work
that you need doing? I can do any work with wool.'

'Why, yes I do,' said the princess, 'I have to wash, comb, card,
spin and weave that big pile of wool into cloth before the giant
comes home, or I dread to think what he will do to me.'

'I can do that for you,' said the tiny yellow-haired boy.

'I can't pay you for the work though,' said the princess.

'All I ask for payment is that you tell me my name when I am
finished.'

The princess thought that this was a good deal and the boy took
all the wool away.

Later in the day an old woman came knocking at the door
looking for a place to stay for the night. The princess had to
turn her away, saying that this was not her house but that of a
giant. She asked the old woman what news she had, but the old
woman said that she had nothing to tell and left the house. The
old woman saw a large mound nearby the house and she lay down

under the sheltered side of it. It felt strangely warm to her and she started to crawl up the slope towards the top, where it was warmest. She saw a light coming from within the mound and she peeped through a crack in the top and saw a whole lot of tiny yellow-headed people all working wool, while a tiny yellow-haired boy ran around, singing:

Tease, teasers, tease;
Card, carders, card;
Spin, spinners, spin;
For Peerie Fool,
Peerie fool is my name.

The old woman returned to the house in the hope of getting lodgings and she told the princess what she had seen. The princess kept saying over and over to herself, 'Peerie Fool. Peerie Fool. Peerie Fool.'

Later that evening the tiny yellow-haired boy came in with the woven cloth and asked the princess to tell him his name. She pretended not to know, giving him the wrong answer, which set him dancing around the floor with delight, saying, 'No, no, no!'

Then she looked him in the eyes and said, 'Peedie Fool is your name!'

The little boy threw the cloth onto the floor with rage and ran out of the house. Just then the giant came home and saw a whole lot of tiny yellow-haired people staggering around, some had their eyes hanging out on their cheeks, some had their tongues hanging down on their breasts; they were a terrible sight to see. The giant asked them what had happened to them and they said that they were exhausted from working wool and weaving it so fine. The giant thought of the princess and said that if she was all right then he would never make her work again. He was relieved to find her sitting happily by the fire with all the wool woven into fine cloth. After that he treated her better and gave her no more tasks to perform.

The next day the youngest princess was cleaning the house when she found her two sisters hanging over the rafters among the hens. She took them down and pulled their skin back over their heels, up their backs and right up to the crown of their heads and they were as right as rain again. Then she hid the eldest princess in the big straw basket and filled it with a lot of the giant's treasure, which he had stolen over the years. Once it was nearly full she covered her sister over with grass to hide her. When the giant came home she asked him to take the basket of grass to her mother, for her cow to eat. The giant agreed and took the basket back to her mother's house. The next day she filled another basket with treasure and put her middle sister on top of it and covered her over with grass too. She got the giant to take this grass to her mother's house for her cow. The next day she told the giant that she had to go away and so would be home late, but could he take a final basket of grass to her mother's house, for her cow. He agreed and left as usual. The youngest princess filled up the basket with the last of the treasure and got on top of it, covering herself over with grass. When the giant took the last basket to the queen's house she had prepared a big pot of boiling water and when the giant arrived they poured it over his head from an upstairs window and that was the end of the giant.

The next story is a Scottish Travellers' tale that was told by an old Orkney Traveller. I am indebted to my friend Jess Smith for giving me this tale and for her kindness in allowing me to write it down here for the first time. Jess is a well-known bestselling writer, singer and storyteller. I would love to say that I heard this story from her as we had a dram by a roaring fire on the seashore under a blanket of stars, but it was actually via a conversation on

Facebook! She asked if I knew this story, which I didn't, so she gave me the bones of it to flesh out. She heard it as a little girl by the fireside of a Travellers' camp from an old piper from Orkney called Newlands. It has all the hallmarks of a Traveller story and is different from the usual Orkney folk tales, having a more West Highlands feel about it. But the Travellers were very active in Orkney, trading goods and working on farms, and they carried with them a huge wealth of stories that are now sadly lost; as Jess said, what remains are only 'the tip of the iceberg'. The magical properties of the seaweed in this story have a remarkable similarity to the dulse that grows at Geo Odin in Stronsay, which, when taken with water from the Well of Kildinguie, was said to cure every illness except the Black Death.

The Kelpie's Seaweed

A mermaid had a child with a human lover, but to her great distress she found that the child could not breathe under water. She carried her little baby boy to a geo[30] where a cave had been cut into the cliffs by the sea and which had a bit of beach in front of it so it was safe and dry. There she placed her son and, with many bitter tears, she left him to live in the realm of mortal men and women. To protect him and look after him she brought a great, black horse, a kelpie, from the depths of the sea. The kelpie, as they are called, had the appearance of a beautiful, sleek horse with a coat as black as jet. This fine, strong horse loved the boy and took great care of him until he was grown into a handsome young man.

His mermaid mother also brought a special, magical seaweed from deep under the ocean and she sprinkled it in a secret place that only the young man and his horse knew. The seaweed thrived and grew there and was gathered by the young man and his kelpie horse. They then took it around the island, selling it to the local farmers who soon discovered that this seaweed had magical properties. Notwithstanding the fact that it tasted delicious the seaweed could cure all ills. It restored the sight to blind eyes and brought the sweet sound of a loved one's voice to ears that had long been deaf. Bald men rubbed it on their shiny domes and soon had a fine, thick crop of hair. Ladies who wanted to lose a few pounds ate it and in no time the fat had disappeared. It was hailed as a miracle and the man and his horse was welcome wherever he went. In fact, people now flocked to him in the hope of curing whatever troubled them.

The years passed by and the young man grew old and grey, but the horse remained the same as it had ever been. No one knew where he came from or where he lived and no one knew where the wonderful seaweed grew, although many had tried to find it. The one thing that never changed was the great bond of love that existed between the man and his horse. People often commented that the two seemed inseparable; you would never see the one without the other. Wherever they went the horse had baskets of seaweed fastened to its side and the people always welcomed them both with gratitude and friendly hospitality.

One day two thieves followed the old man back to his secret home. They were cunning and wicked men who wanted to know where the source of the magical seaweed was. They were careful to keep out of sight and eventually they saw him climb down the cliffs towards the geo where he lived. They lay there for the rest of the day until it was dark and then they headed for the cliff edge. The path that led to the geo was narrow and slippery so that the men were in fear of their lives, but greed drove them on. When they reached the bottom they found the cave and saw that the old man was alone. They seized him and beat him, demanding to know where he got the seaweed from. The old man stood up to this torture for a while until, with a knife pressed hard against his throat, he told them that he didn't

know the answer to their question; it was only the horse who knew the secret place where the magical seaweed grew. They told him to call his horse and he made a loud, piercing whistle. In no time at all the beautiful black horse appeared in the cave mouth and calmly trotted in. The old man whispered into the horse's ear, 'Take the visitors home.'

The two thieves climbed up onto the back of the black horse, triumphant that they would now find the source of the seaweed and be rich men. But this was no ordinary horse; it was a kelpie, a water horse with supernatural powers. The horse galloped out of the cave and over the waves at such speed that the men screamed with terror. It rose up into the night sky, higher and higher it went and the men screamed louder and louder. When the kelpie was so high that they seemed to be able to touch the stars the kelpie gave a flick of its hind legs and the two thieves were tossed from its back and fell to their deaths in the ocean, far below them. The kelpie then returned to the old man to treat his injuries. But it was too late. The old man had suffered so much terror at the hands of the cruel and evil men that his heart was broken in two. He died as the sun rose the following morning.

An old fisherman who had moored his boat near to the hidden cave that day told of a strange sight that he had seen. A great black horse with a mane and tail of greenie-brown kelp stood at the shore and on its back there sat a beautiful woman holding the body of an old man in her arms. The horse then walked slowly into the sea until there was no sight of it or the rider to be seen. People laughed at him when he told them what he saw, but he swore on the Bible that he had seen this remarkable sight. He would later add that he sometimes saw, in the same place, a beautiful black horse walking from the sea and an old man walking on the waves beside it.

Children were told this story with the warning, 'Never take what is not yours to take, or else he'll come for you; the Kelpie Horse!'

8

WITCHES

Orkney had a reputation among sailors as a dangerous place to voyage because of the number of witches who made a living by luring ships onto the rocks. The folk tale collector, Walter Traill Dennison (born in 1825), recalled a strange incident when he was on a visit to Leith as a small boy. An old sailor took him on his knee and told him wonderful tales about the sea, but when he heard that the boy was from Orkney he recoiled, saying, 'O, my lad, you hail from that lubber land where so many cursed witches dwell.'

When he was grown up he had in his collection of antiquities part of the staff of a Sanday witch called 'Ship Maggie'. Here are a couple of stories that he recorded about her.

⋘ SHIP MAGGIE ⋙

Ship Maggie was a notorious witch in eighteenth-century Sanday. She always carried a long staff with her and wore on her feet a pair of rivlins, which was the usual mode of shoes in those days. But what made Ship Maggie's rivlins different was that they were not the usual brown colour of untanned hide, for the left one was white and the right one was black. She got her nickname 'Ship

Maggie' from her power to raise storms and cast ships ashore at her will.

On Tuesday, 22 April 1788 the large whaling ship, *Earl of Chatham*, on her way to Greenland from London, was hit by a raging storm. Captain Peterson and his crew battled to save their lives as the ship pitched and tossed on the foaming seas, but they had no control over her. She went ashore on the Sands of Erraby; a thin spit of sand that juts out into the Bay of Newark in Sanday. The following morning the ship's mate saw Maggie with her white rivlin standing on the shore. He called for a gun, saying, 'I'll shoot that damned hag! I saw her and her white shoe on the foretop before the ship struck.'

One night the tenant of Newark gave Ship Maggie a good present as she went around the houses begging for food. She was very much surprised by the generosity of the farmer and smiled, saying to him, 'You'll be well paid by this time tomorrow.'

That night the winds rose to a howling gale and before the evening of the following day there were three ships wrecked on the sands of the Bay of Newark.

When Ship Maggie's life was drawing to a close she instructed her family that she was to be buried with her staff. The staff was longer than Maggie was and it wouldn't fit in the coffin, so the end was cut off it to make it fit. This piece was later given to Walter Traill Dennison as a memento of this storm-raising witch.

✏ THE STORM WITCH ✏

One beautiful July day in 1627 Benjamin Garrioch and his three friends were preparing their boat for sea. They were young Westray men and Westray always had a reputation for producing the finest sailors. They were going fishing and conditions could not have been better for them. Then Benjamin saw his girlfriend, Janet Forsyth, coming along the beach towards them. She drew Benjamin aside and said to him, 'Don't go to the fishing today Benjie.'

'Why ever not?' he asked.

'I can't tell you, just please don't go.'

The more he questioned her, the more upset she got until she said, 'Last night I had a dream that if you go to sea today then I'll never see you again.'

The young man laughed and, waving his arm towards the sea and sky said, 'Look at it! Not a ripple on the sea and not a cloud in the sky. What could possibly go wrong?'

The tears were streaming down her face as she said, 'Don't leave me Benjie!'

And with that she turned around and ran away along the beach. Benjamin stood and looked confused; Janet had blown hot and cold with him for some time and he never knew where he stood, but he had never seen her like this before. He turned to his friends, shrugged his shoulders and then pushed the boat down to the sea and sailed away. They were never seen again in the island of Westray.

For what can go wrong at sea on a beautiful summer's day? Fog! It rolled in, swallowing up everything in its path and the young men were lost in it too. If that wasn't bad enough, Janet's father died soon after, leaving her alone in the world. All he left was a small tumbled-down cottage and a boat in a noust by the shore. Janet became withdrawn and shunned people's company, sometimes siting in her house for days on end without ever crossing the threshold. Some boys became curious and climbed onto the roof of her house to peep inside. There were no windows in Janet's house and the only light that got in was through the smoke hole in the roof. The boys saw Janet sitting by the fire, her arms wrapped around herself, rocking gently back and fore and singing a lament to herself. People started to whisper about the strange, lonely girl. They became suspicious.

One night the wind started to rise and soon it howled around the houses like a hungry animal. Janet Forsyth was seen leaving her home and heading towards her father's boat. She managed to drag it down to the sea and launched it into the waves. Soon the frail little boat was seen battling its way through the savage seas. It looked like suicide to the folk of Westray; there was no way that a boat could survive such mountainous waves. But it did, and Janet returned home, pulled the boat back to the noust and returned to her lonely home. After that, whenever there was a storm, Janet would set off in her father's little boat and be at sea when it was at its height.

When people talked about Janet Forsyth a new word started to be used and that word was 'witch'.

'Well, she must be a witch. Why; didn't she say that Benjamin Garrioch and his pals would be lost at sea? Sure enough, that's what happened! And how could she survive taking out that small boat into a storm?'

'She must raise the storms.'

'Aye! She's in league with the Devil and she communes with him during the storms that she raises.'

So, poor Janet Forsyth was known as the Westray Storm Witch after that. She did know herbal remedies for sickness so when people were ill they would go to her for a cure. But, of course, when anything became ill it was Janet who got the blame. If a cow stopped milking or a horse went lame it was laid at the door of the Storm Witch.

Things came to a head one day when a particularly terrible storm raged, whipping the sea up into a seething cauldron of foam. A ship had been caught by the strong currents that swirl around Westray and it was being driven towards the rocks. The people gathered on the shore to watch, expecting a rich harvest from the sea. Janet joined them and saw what was happening, but she knew that there was no point in asking anyone if they were going to try to help. She ran down to the noust and pulled the boat down to the raging sea. It was not easy for her to launch it against the breakers, but she managed to somehow. The people looked on in disbelief; surely there was no way that her frail little boat could survive in such seas as this. Slowly they saw the boat climb up a huge wave only to plunge down the other side and disappear from view. Well, surely she has gone this time, they thought, but there it was, climbing another huge wave before plunging into the watery depths once more.

On the ship the captain and crew were frantic, trying to save their ship from being torn to pieces on the rocks. Janet managed to get alongside the ship and secure her boat before climbing on the deck. She started to shout orders to the crew, who were so amazed to see her that they sprang to action immediately. Janet was a fisherman's daughter and she knew all the rocks and currents around the shore as well, if not better, than anyone else. She used the current to turn the ship, taking it away from the dangerous skerries[31] that threatened to tear its hull open. Under Janet's directions they managed to bring the ship safely to anchor in Pierowall Bay. The captain didn't know what to say to her, but he offered her a small gift of a bag of money. Janet looked at him sadly and said, 'Thank you, but I don't want any money from you.

You see, I once had a love who was a sailor and he disappeared. I would like to think that if he was in danger on the sea then someone would help him in his hour of peril.'

With that she returned to her boat and sailed it back to the noust and went home to sit by her fireside and sing her sad songs once more.

These days you would get a medal for such an act of bravery, but not in those days. Janet Forsyth was accused of witchcraft and arrested on the authority of the Church. She was brought to Kirkwall to stand trial in St Magnus Cathedral, where she was held in an unlit cell known as 'Marwick's Hole'. Who Marwick was we do not know but the entrance to the hole that was named after her is through a trapdoor in the floor. The bottom of the cell is dome shaped, like the bottom of a champagne bottle, with sharp, jagged stones set on edge. Here Janet was held for three weeks before her trial.

At the trial her neighbours gave evidence against her; the usual catalogue of cows not milking and animals and people becoming sick. One man even accused her of bringing on an illness while he was at sea so that he felt terribly sick and had to return to the shore. Seeing her on the beach, he accused her of witchcraft, but she scooped up seawater in a bucket that she was carrying and threw it over him, after which he felt much better. It is laughable, but in 1629 it was enough to have you convicted of witchcraft and the only sentence for that was death.

The judge found Janet guilty as charged of witchcraft. He asked her if there was any reason why he shouldn't pass the death sentence on her, but she just looked at him and said, 'I don't care anymore. Death holds no fear for me for I have done nothing wrong. I have never raised a storm, but when I went to sea in those conditions it was because I had hoped that I'd find my Benjie, who could be in trouble on the sea. If anyone protected me at sea it wasn't the Devil, but God that had his hands around me. But I'm tired of life and I welcome death. So, pass your sentence, for I don't care.'

The judge passed the usual sentence for witchcraft on Janet Forsyth ruling that the following morning she was to have her hands bound behind her back and be taken to the Head of the Loan[32] where she was to be worried at the stake[33] until dead and her body burnt to ashes. The crowd in the cathedral shouted their approval and cheered the verdict. As Janet turned to look at them she suddenly screamed, 'Benjie! Save me Benjie!' and then fell to the ground in a faint.

A man in a sailor's uniform ran over to where she lay, scooped her up in his arms and kissed her. The judge was outraged, saying, 'Young man; if it wasn't for the fact that you are serving in His Majesty's navy I would have you punished for contempt of court. Now, release the prisoner and have her locked up.'

They dragged Janet away, still screaming, 'Save me Benjie!'

That night there was a great celebration in Kirkwall, for the fleet was in town. A squadron of Royal Navy ships had been driven north by strong winds and had anchored in Kirkwall Bay. The officers had been invited ashore by the local dignitaries for cake and wine. As the wine flowed (no doubt joined by smuggled gin and brandy) the town council felt generous and ordered that several barrels of ale should be opened at the Market Cross for the sailors and townspeople to enjoy. All were merry and without a care in the world; apart from poor Janet, of course.

The next day, when Janet was due to be led from the cathedral to the place of execution, there was a large crowd gathered to witness the event. The cathedral bell tolled, the time came and went, but there was still no sign of the witch. The sheriff-depute and the provost went to the condemned cell to see what the delay was and came running out shouting that the witch had escaped. There was great confusion; the hangman and his guards were found to be in a deep sleep and the cell was empty. A search was made, but Janet Forsyth was never seen in Orkney again.

A few years later Bailie Baikie was on his way to London on business when he stopped off in Manchester. As he walked down a street there he saw a shop sign that said 'Benjamin Garrioch'. Thinking that this was an Orkney name he went inside to pay his respects when, to his amazement, he recognised Janet Forsyth, the Westray Storm Witch, behind the counter. He had seen her at her trial, but she was a lot younger and healthier looking now than the last time that he had seen her. On saying her name she called into the back shop and out came Benjie Garrioch, who told him the following story.

That fateful day when Benjie left Westray the boat became lost in the fog. They sailed around for a while, not knowing where to go, when they saw a shape in the distance and headed towards it. On getting near they saw to their horror that it was a Royal Navy man-o'-war. They were seized and pressed into the navy and carried off to fight in the war against France, as was the fate of so many young Orkney men over the years. The ship he was on was driven north with the rest of the squadron and anchored in Kirkwall Bay. This was his first time back in Orkney since being pressed, so he went ashore and strolled through the narrow streets of Kirkwall before seeing people going into the cathedral. He and some of the sailors followed them and saw that there was a witch trial taking place, little knowing who it was that was on trial. He cheered at the verdict along with the rest of them, but then to his horror saw that the condemned woman was his Janet. He decided that he must save her; but how? He carried cogs of ale to the hangman and the two men who guarded Janet's cell, knowing that they had a reputation for drunkenness, but he mixed a sleeping powder into the ale and soon they were dead to the world. He got Janet out and they hurried on the road to the east and over the brae to Inganess Bay where the ship that Janet had saved was lying at anchor. The captain and crew wanted to help her, as they owed her their lives, and so she was soon safely on board. Benjamin returned to his ship, so as not to arouse suspicion, while the ship carrying Janet sailed south to Liverpool. She stayed there with the captain's wife and family until Benjamin was able to desert his ship at Portsmouth and join up with her. With what money he had, plus a bit from the captain, they moved to Manchester where they started their own business. Bailie Baikie was amazed to hear this story and promised not to tell a soul; but I suppose he must have, otherwise I couldn't tell it to you now. So, there are descendants of Janet Forsyth, the Westray Storm Witch, living in Manchester to this day.

How much truth there is in that story is hard to say. Janet Forsyth did exist and she was sentenced to death for witchcraft in 1629, but as far as Benjamin Garrioch and the rescue are concerned it could just be a Victorian invention. However, there were a very high number of witches executed in Orkney in this dark period of our history. The possibility of erecting a memorial to them at the site of the gallows is currently being discussed.

ᙚ MAMMY SCOTT ᙚ

In 1814 Sir Walter Scott, while visiting Stromness with the Northern Lighthouse Board, met a notorious witch called Bessie Millie who had a small cottage on Brinkie's Brae overlooking the town and who sold fair winds to sailors for sixpence a time. She was succeeded by another witch who could control the winds called Mammy Scott. Here are two short stories relating to her.

A captain called at Mammy Scott's house to secure a fair wind for his return voyage to Stornoway in Lewis. She took his money and

gave him a piece of string that had three knots tied in it. He was told to untie the first knot if the wind was not strong enough and to untie the second knot if he required a bit more wind. But on no account was he to untie the third knot, or things would turn out bad for him. He thanked her and set sail on his ship. The wind was light so he untied the first knot and a strong breeze filled the sails meaning the ship made good speed through the Hoy Sound and along the coast of Sutherland. The captain was still not satisfied with the strength of the wind so he undid the second knot. The breeze picked up and started to blow briskly so that the ship made good speed around Cape Wrath and southwards towards the Hebrides. Before long the ship was approaching the entrance to Stornoway Harbour and the captain started to wonder what would happen if he was to untie the third knot. They were home already, so what could possibly go wrong? He untied the third knot and suddenly the wind swung around and blew straight at them, the sky turned black and a hurricane stated to blow. The ship, so close to home, was forced to turn around and run before the gale, all the way back north, through the Hoy Sound and back to Stromness.

In the meantime Mammy Scott had fallen out with a man from Walls and held a grudge against him and his family. She had taken a passage over the Pentland Firth and went to a house in Caithness where she asked if she could rest for an hour or so. It seems that the dispute may have occurred during the voyage across to the Firth; something the Walls man did on a regular basis. Mammy Scott asked the woman of the house if she would fetch her a bucket of water and a 'bummie',[34] which the woman did. Mammy Scott set the bummie floating on the surface of the water then started to stir the water with her finger until the water upset the bummie and it sank. Mammy Scott watched this with a cold look in her eyes and said, 'Aye, there they go; but I'm sorry for the poor stranger laddie that's with them.'

That evening the Walls man and his two sons were drowned in the Pentland Firth, along with a passenger that they were ferrying over, when their boat suddenly capsized for no apparent reason.

∽ SCOTA BESS ∾

The following story was collected by Walter Traill Dennison as a 'here-meed-rhyme'; an old ballad that was based on a folk tale, which went under the title of 'Lady Sarah's Voyage'.

Lady Sarah was the daughter of a wealthy laird who lived in Dundee. Her mother had died when Sarah was only a small child and her father loved her dearly as she looked more and more like his lost love with every passing year. Many rich men's sons tried in vain to win her as their bride, but they were sent away disappointed and crushed. Sarah did not want any of these men, or their love, for she already loved another. She had fallen in love with a brave knight, a soldier who was now fighting the king's foes over the sea and she had promised him faithfully that she would wait for his return. But the time passed by and she was still alone in her father's house until eventually her heart grew weary of waiting.

A brave sea Rover heard of Lady Sarah's beauty and he vowed that he would win her heart, no matter what it took. He courted her in secret, using sweet words that flowed from his lips like poisoned honey. He was bold and brave and had amassed a great fortune. He told her stories of all the places that he had been, all the wonders of the world that he had seen, and slowly, but surely, he started to win her over. He told her that her brave knight had forgotten about her and was spending his days in revelry, wine and song while she withered away in her father's house. He said that her knight was courting other women and had forgotten about his childish vow to her. She should forget that false knight and come away on his ship where they would sail to the West Indies and live in paradise. And so it was arranged that on a certain night he would come for her and that they would run away together and be happy for the rest of their days.

On the appointed day her father was in a sad mood. His life was never happy since the day that his dear wife passed away, for the pain had never left his heart. He called to his daughter to sing to him before he went to bed. Her song was as melancholy as his mood; a lament that tore at his heart. He thanked her, saying that he saw in her the sadness that was within him, but that he hoped that her knight would return safely from the wars soon and then her days would be filled with laughter and light. On hearing this Sarah went to her bedchamber and threw herself on the bed, weeping for her lost love and the father that she would never see again if she was to leave that night. Her old nurse tried to comfort her, but she sent her away. Then her maidservant came in; a girl whose loyalty had been bought by the Rover and who was to try to turn her mistress against her life there. She whispered lies into Lady Sarah's ear, saying that she had heard it said that her father was planning to send her to a French convent to become a nun and to live alone for the rest of her life. She said too that she had heard that her brave knight was now married in London and had never intended to return to her. These lies found a home in Sarah's heart and they grew there like a cancer in her soul.

At the appointed hour she heard a knock on her window and her maidservant opened it to let the Rover in. They made ready and left; both Lady Sarah and her maidservant took horses and rode to the docks where their ship awaited them. They cast off at once and sailed south on the first leg of their journey to the West Indies. But as they reached the coast of Kent the wind veered around and freshened to gale force, blowing the Rover's ship to the north. He ordered that they keep away from land when they drew near to Dundee, in case Lady Sarah should recognise it and want to return to her father. The wind raged on and the ship went further northwards until they reached the Pentland Firth. The pilot advised against trying to find a route through the Firth, as its reputation was fearsome as a graveyard of ships. The pilot also worried about the Orkney witches who raised storms and lured ships to their doom. But the Rover ordered them to sail through the Firth and so they tried their best. The ship pitched and tossed wildly as the currents flowed against them and they could not make any headway.

Suddenly, a beautiful ship passed them by and tried to sail through the Firth. She was painted all over with bright colours and looked like a gem floating on the surface of the sea. This ship battled against the tide, but couldn't get through either, so it turned about and started to sail to the north-east. The Rover admired that beautiful ship and ordered his men to follow her. The pilot said that it was certain death to try to steer a ship through the Orkney Isles, but the Rover said that the painted ship seemed to know the way, so they would follow her. She sailed by Copinsay then north around the Mull Head of Deerness and towards Stronsay and the Rover followed her like a dog follows its master.

In Stronsay lived Scota Bess, a witch who could control the elements, raising both storms and fog at will. She took her seat in the Maiden's Chair that was cut into the rocks of Mill Bay and where, it was said, if a maiden sat she would be given the gift of prophesy. Scota Bess sat in the Maiden's Chair and watched the ships as they sailed to the north and an evil laugh fell from her wrinkled mouth.

'The Devil will sing and be merry tomorrow as he enjoys his sport with the souls of that ship's crew.'

The doomed vessel sailed around Papa Stronsay and into the Sanday Sound, still following the painted ship.

Lady Sinclair sat in her hall at Warsetter in Sanday and watched the Rover's ship pass by. She had the gift of second sight and tears filled her eyes as she said to her maids, 'There is a man-sworn

woman[35] on that stately ship and she is doomed for the sin that she has committed.'

The two ships carried on around Sanday as the sun set. The pilot came to the Rover and said, 'Have you noticed that ship has carried full topgallant-sails throughout the gale but has never been further forward or nearer to us than it appears now? I say we shouldn't follow it any longer, for if we were in the southern seas I'd swear that we were following Vander Dick[36] himself!'

But the Rover was headstrong and swore that he would carry on following that ship as it was their best chance of getting through the islands alive.

'Breakers ahead!' cried the lookout. 'Breakers on the lee bow!'

There before them they could see the broken water with the jagged rocks beneath it. Lady Sarah and her maidservant were on the poop deck with the Rover by this time.

The painted ship that sailed before them suddenly melted away into smoke. A blue flame shot up from the sea where it had been and it was gone. A phantom ship created by witchcraft to lure them to their doom. But from where the flame had been there appeared a boat that glided over the sea towards them. In it were two spectres; one old man with white hair and a young man with raven black locks. The young man spoke, 'Come down to me, Lady Sarah, for our wedding is arranged. The priest is waiting and the feast is ready for us. Remember the vow that you took to be faithful to me? How true have you been? The wedding bed is far away and the wedding night will be long. Hear the surf on the shore; it plays the Death March for you tonight. Join me, my love, in the land of the dead.'

Then the old man spoke to the Rover, 'Proud Rover; you have wronged me greatly and now you have taken my daughter to her death. You have gathered your wealth by villainy and your pride has corrupted you. You shall never know peace and your soul will burn with anguish so that you would welcome death to free you from its pain. But in death you will suffer still as a cursed and evil man.'

The old man gave his daughter a last look and with tears in his eyes he raised his hand in farewell and then the spectral image vanished from sight. At that moment the ship struck the rocks and a hole was torn in its side. The Rover ordered his men to the pumps, but the water flowed in too fast for them to master it. Some of the crew found the rum and wine that was on board and they drank their fill, deciding that if they were about to die then they would be merry before their time ran out.

The maidservant stood before the Rover and cursed him to his face, 'You lied to her, and to me. You've doomed us all to die by your greed and pride. I know well what you are! A pirate, a low-life buccaneer who stole everything he has. May the Devil curse you and torment you in the deepest pit of hell.'

The ship lurched, stuck fast on the Yarrow Bank in Sanday and started to break into pieces. Lady Sarah stood by the side of the Rover as the ship was torn to pieces around them. She had made her peace with God and said her farewell to the man who had deceived her and wrought her destruction. He grabbed her and jumped into the sea; holding her tightly with his left hand he struck for the shore using his right one. The sea was wild and the current strong as he tried to reach the shore, being pulled back by the sea when he got near to land. Eventually he reached the shore and collapsed in a faint. When he recovered his senses he could see Lady Sarah's face in the moonlight next to him. Her hand still grasped his arm, but she was already dead. He looked at her pale face in the moon's beams and kissed her cold, wet lips a last goodbye. Inside he felt his heart break and his spirit bend, like it had never done before. With the first light he saw the carnage on the sea-strand as heads and limbs were washed ashore among the seaweed. Dead eyes stared at him accusingly, and they seemed to say, 'This was all your doing.'

Among the mangled corpses, ship's timbers, sailcloth and ropes were the remains of the Rover's treasure. A white damask cloth was found and he used this as a shroud for his lady. A golden girdle was fastened around her waist and he carried her to the shore where she was to be buried. Of the crew only one man survived. The rest were laid in graves by the Yarrow Knowes[37] and Lady Sarah was laid in a grave where the daisies now grow over her. The Rover wandered the earth for the rest of his days, a haunted man with a tormented soul who was doomed to enjoy none of life's pleasures in this life or the next.

Scota Bess was a real Stronsay witch who was said to be able to raise a thick sea fog and phantom ships to lure the unwary onto the rocks. She was murdered by a group of men around the year 1630. They had somehow lured her to the barn at Huip and then beat her to death using flails that had been washed in what they believed was holy water (the water had been used to rinse out the communion cup at the local church). She was buried in a nearby field, but in the morning her body was found lying on the surface. The following night they took her body to a loch in the middle of the island called Meikle Water and dumped it there before carrying boatloads of earth and stones to the spot to cover her with. They used so much material that they created an island in the loch, which can still be seen to this day. One interesting fact is that a few years ago I had the pleasure of hosting the Icelandic writer and journalist, Þorgrímur Gestsson, who was researching an historical travel book based on the Icelandic Sagas. One night, as we chatted by the fire, he told me that he was interested in old Nordic words and while he was in the far north of Norway he heard the word *skodda*, which meant a sea fog. He checked it out on his return home and found that it was used in both Norway and Iceland. Could 'Scota Bess' actually be 'skodda Bess', meaning 'foggy Bess'? I rather think so.

✆ THE BATTLE OF SUMMERDALE ✆

The Battle of Summerdale in the summer of 1529 was the last pitched battle fought on Orkney soil. It was a dispute about the inheritance of the Earldom of Orkney, more an inter-family squabble than anything else. King James V had to stamp his authority on this unruly and relatively new addition to Scotland, so he sent an army to Orkney led by John Sinclair, Earl of Caithness (and kinsman of the feuding Sinclair earls of Orkney). The invasion fleet sailed into Scapa Flow, but a thick fog made them lose their way so instead of landing at Scapa Bay and marching towards Kirkwall they landed at a beach in Orphir, probably Waulkmill Bay. On landing they found a witch waiting for them. She held a ball of coloured wool in each hand, one blue and one red, which she unwound as she marched up and down before them. The ball of red wool ran out first and she declared that the first blood to be spilled would be on the losing side. Determined to give his men a good omen the earl ordered them to seize a herd boy who was on the hillside and bring him down to the beach. The trembling boy was brought to the earl who drew his sword and killed him on the spot. The old witch shook her head and said, 'That's a bad thing that you've done, for that was not an Orcadian but a Caithness boy who came here to live last year with his mother.'

When the earl's men heard this they started to murmur that this didn't bode well, but the earl ordered them to march onwards. They passed the Kirbister Loch and ended up, not in Kirkwall as they had intended, but in the valley of Summerdale near the boundary of the parishes of Orphir and Stenness. Here the Orkney men were waiting for them in ambush, their spies having kept a close watch on their enemy's movements. A fierce battle ensued, in which the Earl of Caithness was killed. The Orkney men had divine help, as a cross appeared in the sky above the battlefield and St Magnus himself was seen fighting on their side. Stones also miraculously appeared at the Orkney men's feet, ready to be thrown at the invading Scots.

By the end of the battle all the Caithness men were killed and not a single Orcadian had fallen in battle. In fact, there was only one casualty on the Orkney side and that was not as a result of the fighting. He was a poor crofter who lived with his mother in a small house called Tuskerbister[38] up on the side of the hill. After the battle was over he went down to the battlefield and started to strip the bodies of the dead Caithness men. He dressed himself up in their fine clothes and returned home. His mother saw a stranger approaching the house, dressed in a strange fashion, and she thought it was a Caithness man. She went inside and took a woollen stocking and filled it with stones. When the stranger walked through the door she struck him on the head, killing him instantly. Imagine her shock when she recognised the body of her own son lying dead on the floor before her.

✑ TAKING THE PROFIT OF MILK ✑

Witches were always trying to steal the profit from their neighbours' cows so that they got the creamy milk while their neighbour got nothing but thin, watery fluid that was useless. There are so many stories of this kind, but I will only tell one here.

A young man in Birsay was looking for work as a farmhand and was given the job as a cow man on a large farm. After a short time the cows stopped giving milk and the grieve[39] became suspicious. He called the cow man to him and asked if he had seen anyone or anything strange paying attention to the cattle. The man thought and said, 'Well, yes; there was an old woman who came to the field and called to the cows and they all came running up to her. She talked to them and petted them for a while and then left.'

'Ah ha!' said the grieve. 'That's her; she's a witch and has taken the profit from our cows. But I know how to beat her at her own game.'

He took down a bottle from a shelf and gave it to the man, saying, 'When one of the cows is pissing hold this bottle under the stream and fill it, then take it back to me.'

The man was puzzled, but he did as he was told. When a cow pissed he filled the bottle with her water and took it to the grieve who put a cork tightly in the bottle and said, 'There; now we will find out who it is.'

The following day an old woman who lived nearby came to the house in great distress and pain. She knocked on the door and when the grieve opened it she said, 'For mercy sake will you uncork that bottle? I've not been able to piss for a whole day and I feel as if I'm going to die because of it.'

'So, are you the one who has been stealing the profit of my cows?'

'Aye,' muttered the old woman, 'I did indeed.'

'Well,' said the grieve, 'you had better promise to return it and to never interfere with my cows again or the next time I won't uncork the bottle. Do I make myself clear?'

'Aye, aye,' said the old woman, 'as clear as day. I promise never to touch your cows again.'

So the grieve uncorked the bottle and the old woman was relieved in an instant. Never again did she try to steal the profit from those cows.

My mother, who came from Westray, once told me that her father, Geordie Drever, lost the profit of his best cow to a witch in the years between the wars. He had a cow that was a great milker and when she had a calf the thick, creamy milk was excellent for making butter and cheese. One day this old woman came to visit, saying that she had heard about his cow who gave such a lot of good milk and she asked to see it. My grandfather was reluctant to let her in the byre as her reputation for witchcraft was well known. But she pressed him and nagged him until in the end he took her to see the cow. She admired the cow, stroking her hand up and down her back and muttering, 'What a bonnie cow; what a fine cow.'

After that she would not give a drop of milk. He went to see a neighbour who advised him to sell the cow, as this was the only way that the spell would be broken. He sold the cow and she started to give milk again just as well as she ever did.

9

THE DEVIL

⟨ THE LAIRD AND THE DEVIL ⟩

Thomas Traill of Holland, Papa Westray (1668–1694) was known simply as 'the wicked laird', a reputation he richly deserved. To many of these early lairds their tenants were little more than livestock to do with as they pleased. The Traills of Holland claimed the right of the virginity of their crofters' daughters, taking the frightened girl from her wedding feast to satisfy the laird's lust. But Thomas, it was said, was in league with the Devil; not only that, it was said that he was so evil that he had beaten the Devil at his own game.

Thomas Traill had indeed sold his soul to the Devil and the contract came to an end. One day, as Traill sat at his leisure, the Devil appeared before him and said, in a very formal and well-educated voice.

'Well Thomas; I believe that you have something belonging to me that is now ready to be – harvested.'

'Oh, I don't think so,' said the laird, 'I'm quite happy where I am and am not in a hurry to change my circumstances.'

A black looked crossed the Devil's face, as he was not used to being argued with or treated so lightly.

'Now, come on,' he demanded, 'a deal is a deal and your time is up!'

But the wicked laird could not be persuaded to come peaceably and the two started to fight. Their battle was said to have taken place at a field called the 'West Park'. In the end the wicked laird drove the Devil down through the ground and since that day not a blade of grass or as much as a weed has grown on that spot.

Now free of the Devil the wicked laird continued his persecution of the tenants who lived on his island. Every year the crofters, who rented small farms from the laird, and the cottars, who lived on pieces of poor-quality land and paid their rent in labour, brought their sheep in from the common grazing to shear them. At that time the laird would ride up on his horse and select the finest lamb as a gift for his lady wife. One year his eyes fell on a fine grey lamb that he considered to be better than the others. He ordered that the lamb be brought up to the big house immediately. The owner of the lamb was a poor cottar widower who had two small children to support on his own. He begged the laird to be merciful, 'Please, sir, spare me my lamb. It's the only thing that I have in the world and is the only hope of keeping life in me and my bairns over the coming winter. Take another lamb, but spare mine, for the sake of God.'

The laird fixed him with a look of contempt, saying, 'I don't care whether you or your brats live another winter or not! I want that lamb for my lady and that is final.'

Seeing starvation staring him and his children in the face the cottar pulled himself up to his full height and uttered this curse, 'All right, take the lamb; but I'll tell you this. Your lady will never live to see that lamb and when you die you will go to your grave without a drop of blood in your body!'

The wicked laird just laughed in the cottar's face and then turned his horse for home. On arriving at the big house he dismounted his horse and strode inside. He shouted to his wife, but there was no reply. He went upstairs to her bedroom and found her lying dead on the bed. Her body was contorted and her face twisted in horror. The cottar was right – she would never see the lamb.

The years passed and the laird grew in size, as well as in evil reputation, until he finally gasped his last. A huge coffin had to be built; it was said that it took eight score of nails to fasten it together. His remains were laid in the coffin and he lay in state in the hall of the big house for his peers to see him. If anyone had a good word to say about him then it escaped them at that time for no one had any fond memories of him. But there was food and drink aplenty and so they came from all over Orkney. As they gathered in the hall on the day of the funeral they heard a strange, scuffling, scratching sound coming from the chimney breast. Suddenly, two immense ravens burst out of the fireplace and flew around the room, uttering terrible croaks. The two ravens landed on the lid of the coffin and started to fight, but the people shooed them off so that they flew to the mantelpiece and continued the fight there. People were sure that this was the soul of the laird and the Devil, gripped in mortal combat.

They lifted the coffin and started to carry it towards the kirkyard to lay him to rest with his ancestors. The two ravens flew out of the door and circled over the coffin as it went, still tearing at each other with beak and claws. As they walked along the road they saw it; a drip – drip – drip of blood coming from the coffin. They sent a servant back to the house to get a spade to cover the blood with dusty earth, but it was no use. The further they went the worse it got. The drip turned into a trickle, which turned into a pour until blood was running freely from the coffin. By the time that they got the wicked laird to his grave there would not have been a drop of blood left in his body, and so the cottar's curse had come true.

❧ THE BOOK OF THE BLACK ARTS ❧

Where the Book of the Black Arts came from, no one knows, but it was said that it was written in hell by the Devil. It was written in white letters on black pages and contained spells that gave the owner great power, but it came at a price. If you died with the book in your possession then the book, and you, would be claimed by the author and you would suffer a special torment in the deepest, darkest pits of hell.

There was an old woman in Sanday called Rachael who had sold herself to the Devil long ago and was the proud owner of a copy of the Book of the Black Arts, but as her days drew to an end she was keen to be rid of it. However, this was not as easy as you might think for you could not give it away but you had to sell it to someone who agreed to accept it. Moreover the price was a silver coin of a lesser value than the one that you had bought it for.

A local crofter had fallen out with old Rachael and was suddenly taken ill. His teenage daughter, Jessie, suspected witchcraft, but didn't know what to do to save her father. She slipped quietly out

of the house and went to see old Rachael, who didn't give her a
very friendly reception.

'Please,' said the trembling girl, 'I have come to beg you to spare
my father's life. I know that things are not good between you, but
don't take him from us. I couldn't bear to lose him and would do
anything to save him.'

A look of cunning crossed old Rachael's face and she said.

'Aye, there is something that you can do to save your father.
I have an old book here that I want to be rid of. Buy it from me
and I'll spare your father.'

'I don't have much money,' said Jessie.

'I only want a silver threepenny bit for it.'

Old Rachael's eyes glowed in their sunken sockets as the girl
took out her purse and gave her the coin. The strange book was
thrust into her bosom and she was told to leave. Jessie ran home,
her heart pounding as she clutched the book to her breast. She
hid it in the barn before going inside to see how her father was. To
her delight he seemed to be a bit better and it soon became clear
that he was well on the road to recovery. But there was still the
matter of the strange book. Jessie took it from its hiding place and
brought it inside, when no one was around. She sat on her bed and
opened the pages. A vile stench seemed to rise from it as her eyes
scanned the strange white words written on the coal-black pages.
It was in an antique style of writing and some of the words were
unknown to Jessie but she got the gist of their meaning. There was
nothing good in this book; it was pure evil. The spells were not
about getting a handsome young man to fall in love with you, or
giving good luck to anyone, but about spite and hate. How to kill
animals, cause crops to fail, bring sickness and death on people and
how to raise storms or capsize a boat at sea. Jessie shuddered as she
read the words. She had to destroy this evil thing.

She tore at the pages, but they would not rip out; it was as if they
were made of iron. She took it to the fireplace and tossed it into the

fire, but it just lay there among the flames, mocking her. After a while, when it became obvious that the book wouldn't burn, Jessie picked it up with the fire tongs, placing it on the hearth. To her amazement it was stone cold and not so much as singed by the fire. She slipped the cursed book into a sack and went to the cliffs on the south end of the island. Putting stones in the bottom of the sack she tied its mouth and threw it into the sea. It made a loud splash as it entered the water. But when Jessie returned home she found the book was back before her, lying on her bed, waiting to be used. She took a spade and went away where it was quiet and she wouldn't be seen and she dug a hole and put the book into it and covered it over. She saw it's black leather cover disappear beneath the soil and sand of the island. But on her return there was the book, lying on her bed, waiting to be used.

There was nothing that Jessie could do to be rid of that book and she started to become ill at the thought of it. Eventually she went to see the minister, the Reverend Mathew Armour.[40] When he

heard about the book he grew angry that such an abomination should exist in his parish, but when Jessie explained how she had come by it he softened.

'I have to buy this from you, as I believe that is how it's done, for a silver coin of lesser value that the one that you bought it for.'

Jessie burst into tears, saying, 'But I paid a silver threepenny bit for it. There is no silver coin of a lesser value than that.'

'Come now,' said the minister, 'there is always a way.'

He pulled open a drawer and rummaged around inside it until he found an old coin.

'Here,' he said, triumphantly, 'this is an antique silver coin of lesser value that your one. Take it and bring that abominable book to me.'

Jessie ran home to fetch the book and brought it to the manse, where the minister lived. What he did, no one knows, but he must have weakened its power with prayer for he built a big bonfire and burnt it to ashes. It was said that the thick, black, acrid smoke blackened the sky around it as it burned, but that was the end of the Book of the Black Arts in Sanday.

It is interesting to note that another copy of the Book of the Black Arts was taken out of circulation by the Reverend Charles Clouston, Church of Scotland minister for Sandwick from 1832–84. He bought the book for a silver coin but never opened it, as he knew that it couldn't exert its full power over you if you didn't open its pages. He buried it in the garden of his manse at Flotterston in Sandwick with a Bible on top of it to fix it. It is said that it is still there.

౼ THE DEVIL'S FINGERMARKS ౻

The Lady kirk stands by the shore in the parish of Lady in the island of Sanday. The ruin of the old kirk stands roofless and windowless, the door blocked up to prevent people from being injured by a possible collapse of its walls. Outside there is a flight of stone stairs leading to the upper gallery or 'loft', which forms the only access to this level. The stairs have a low wall built around them as a protection for the user, but once you reach the top you are greeted with a very unusual sight indeed for there on the balustrade are the marks of the Devil's claws cut deep into the stone. There are two very different stories told about how they got there, which I will share with you here.

The first version that I heard was that there was a new minister in the parish whose sermons were regarded as a wonder to hear. His popularity saw the numbers of worshipers swell until the kirk could hardly contain their numbers. One day the Devil decided to go there to listen to the sermon, to hear for himself whether the minister was as good as they said he was. He climbed the stairs to the loft and listened to the sermon of this gifted preacher. He soon found out that everything that he had heard was indeed true and the rage built up inside of him until he started to scratch his claws along the flagstone capping of the wall, leaving the deep scratches that we can still see to this day.

The second version may be more original and it seems that people are reluctant to repeat it. It was said that there was a minister in Lady Parish who preached on a Sunday against all the things that he himself enjoyed doing during the week; especially adultery. It was known that the minister was having an affair with a married woman in the parish and soon news of this reached the Devil's ears. One night the minister slipped out of the married woman's house and proceeded to head for home. On the way the Devil appeared in front of him and tried to carry him off to hell, but the minister turned and fled for his life. The Devil was in hot pursuit, but the terrified minister, having more to lose than the Devil, ran like a rabbit chased by a dog until he reached the sanctuary of the kirk. Once through the door the minister was safe, as the Devil could not cross the threshold of the kirk. In his rage the Devil looked all around the kirk for a way to grab the wayward minister, but there was nothing. In his rage he tore at the top of the stairs with his claws, leaving his marks behind as testimony of that night's chase.

ஸ் THE DEVIL ON THE RAFTERS ஒ

The Reverend Yule was preaching in St Magnus Cathedral one Sunday when he saw, to his annoyance, a girl who was sitting smiling while he spoke. As his sermon was anything but amusing he felt highly offended by her behaviour. To make matters worse she continued to smile throughout and then at the end she had the audacity to laugh. This was more than he could stand and the offender was ordered to stay back and explain herself. The girl apologised for laughing but explained that she could not help it. She said that while he was preaching she noticed that the Devil was sitting on one of the rafters and he was taking a note of the names of the people who were asleep during the sermon and that had made her smile. The Devil only had one piece of paper and soon he had filled both sides of it. As he still had more names to add to his list he tore the tail off his shirt and started to write on that. Soon he had also filled up both sides of the linen so he held it in his teeth and pulled it in order to stretch it so that he could squeeze on some more names. Once that was also full he tried to stretch it again in the same manner, but the linen couldn't withstand more punishment and it tore, causing the Devil to jerk his head backwards and bang it on the rafter. The old minister now smiled himself and said, 'A wonderful vision; a marvellous vision!'

ஸ் DRINKING WITH THE DEVIL ஒ

Drinking was almost an art form among the Orkney lairds in the seventeenth and eighteenth centuries and smuggled gin from Holland and brandy from France was a feature at these occasions. Punch was served in large bowls; a heady mixture of spirits, hot water and sugar. This story was told by Walter Traill Dennison in his 1880 masterpiece *The Orcadian Sketch Book*. It was contained within another story about the excesses of the landed classes in mid-eighteenth-century Orkney.

Velzian, Scarth, Craigie and Inkster gathered at a large house in Rousay for a drinking session one night. Velzian was famous for his prowess as a heavy drinker and was much admired for it among his friends. They started to pass around the punch bowl, but decided that they would abandon the glasses and just drink straight from the bowl. As the first lot disappeared down their willing throats Velzian decided to up the stakes by dispensing with the hot water and sugar and taking the spirits as God intended them. The bowl was filled and passed around, with the course of the sun, until the men were witless with drink. They made toast after toast, each one saucier than the last, until the drinking reached its crescendo. One by one Scarth, Craigie and Inkster slipped underneath the table as the drink took a hold of them, until only Velzian remained upright. He smiled a big stupid grin, as he cherished his victory at the drinking, but he was sorry that he was now alone and had no one to drink with. Just as he lifted the punch bowl to his head once more he heard a strange sound, like a horse snorting, coming from under the table. He thought that it was one of his friends snoring, but the sound grew louder and louder until it occurred to him that maybe one of them was choking, so he looked under the table to see what was going on. To Velzian's surprise he saw a figure crouched over Craigie with its hands around his throat.

'Here, you ill-mannered bitch[41],' shouted Velzian, 'that's no way to behave in the company of gentlemen. Get up and show yourself, or by the head of St Mans[42] I'll give you a skin full of sore bones!'

There was a flash of light that seemed to come from the stranger's eyes and he slowly rose up to his full height and gave a loud, menacing laugh. The sight of the creature that stood before Velzian would have driven a sober man mad, but luckily Velzian was far from being sober. The man had skin as black as soot, crooked horns grew from his head and white flames darted from his eyes. Velzian knew that he was in the company of the Devil, and that was bad company to find yourself in.

'How dare you speak to me in such a tone,' said the Devil, in a well-educated voice. 'Don't you know who I am?'

'I neither know nor care who you are,' said Velzian, 'I only know that you are an ill-bred scoundrel, coming in here among decent folk in such a fashion. Sit down and drink with me and tell me who you are or I'll give you such a threshing that I'll crush every bone in your body.'

'You're a bold fellow,' said the Devil, 'we'll try the drinking first.'

Velzian drank a toast and then handed the punch bowl to the Devil, who took it and drank deep. When he handed it back to Velzian he noticed that there were sooty fingermarks on the sides of the bowl and a sooty mark where his mouth had been.

'You ill-mannered brute,' roared Velzian, 'how dare you come to the table without washing your hands and face.'

Flames darted from the Devil's eyes and he said, 'Take off your waistcoat and fight me!'

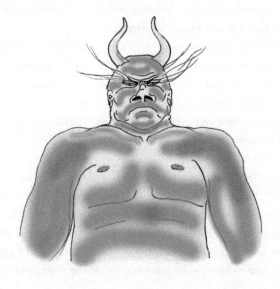

Velzian was drunk, but he wasn't stupid. He knew that his old mother had sewn a few pages from a psalm book into the lining of the waistcoat and as long as he had it on then the Devil had no power over him.

'I'm damned if I will,' said Velzian, 'I think I'm man enough to fight you with my waistcoat on.'

'If you don't take off your waistcoat,' said the Devil, 'then you will soon be lying dead with your friends under the table.'

'Them?' laughed Velzian, 'They're not dead; only dead drunk!'

'Oh, is that so?' said the Devil. 'Well, seeing is believing.'

He picked up Inkster's lifeless body from under the table and threw it over Velzian's knee. He then clapped his hands together until the sparks flew from them. To Velzian's horror he saw the ghosts of his three friends floating behind the Devil, their faces full of terror and they seemed to be pleading, 'Help us, Velzian; help us!'

Velzian was so shocked that fear gripped him for a moment. He tried to say a blessing, but he found that the Devil had such power in the room that he could not utter the word 'God'. But he realised that there was no time for fear now and that he had to have his wits about him if he was to save his friends.

'Well, you are a clever man all right,' said Velzian, 'but then again any fool can knock the soul out of a drunk man, but it would be another thing to put the soul back in the body again.'

The Devil smiled and said, 'Oh, I can do that too. In fact, I'll do it right now if you swear to take off your waistcoat and fight me once I've completed it.'

'It's a deal!' said Velzian.

The Devil picked up Scarth's body and, grabbing a quivering ghost from behind him, he thrust it back inside, just like putting a pig in a poke. As he was busy doing that Velzian was unpicking the seam of his waistcoat and drew out one of the pages from the psalm book. He pulled the bung out of the small keg of gin that stood next to him on the table and poked the page inside before sealing it again. He thought that he would never do it in time, but the Devil made the mistake of trying to put Craigie's soul into Scarth's body and he found that it wouldn't fit. This delayed him for long enough for Velzian to finish his work. Once their souls were back in their bodies his three friends stood there alive again.

'Now take off your waistcoat and fight me,' said the Devil.

'I never said when I'd take off my waistcoat,' said Velzian, 'now get out of this house, you ill-bred muckle black whalp, in God's name!'[43]

Velzian picked up the keg of gin and threw it with all its might at the Devil's head. The keg burst to pieces against his horns and he let out a wild yell and flew up the chimney in a blue flame.

'Velzian; if ever I get my hands on you you'll burn in brimstone for all time!' he cried out, but it was noticed that his fine English had left him and he now spoke in Orcadian dialect.[44]

Velzian's friends were shaken by their experience and had sobered up pretty fast as well. They thanked their friend for saving them, saying, 'Velzian, you've baptised the Devil in gin, seasoned with a psalm book.'

Velzian laughed and said, 'Aye, but I don't think he liked the seasoning.'

ঞ্চ SATI ঞ্চ

Sati lived with his wife in a small house in the hills between Orphir and Stenness around 1700. His name was a nickname as he claimed to be a great wizard who had his knowledge from Satan himself. His speciality was finding stolen items, especially money. This reputation was what got him by and put food on the table and this reputation was all that he had to go on. Whenever there was a theft the victim would make the long journey up the hill to Sati's house, up a trail that was observed by the residents. Sati would then hide in a specially concealed room, little bigger than a cupboard, which had a secret door leading outside. His wife would welcome the visitor, but tell them that Sati was not at home at that moment but was expected back soon. As they waited Sati's wife would pump them for information as to what was lost, when it went missing and if anyone had been seen around the house at the time that it disappeared. Sati would be listening to all of this and when all the information was extracted he would slip out of the secret door and make a dramatic entrance, saying that he knew who was waiting to see him and the reason that brought them there. He would give such precise details of the loss that the listener was amazed to hear it. Sati would then tell them to go home and to let everyone know that he knew full well who had committed the crime and that if the missing goods were not returned by the following morning then he would expose the culprit in front of the whole neighbourhood. As soon as the guilty party heard this the goods were always returned and Sati would receive payment; his reputation intact!

But Sati nearly lost everything one day when his usual scheme didn't go to plan. In the district of Tenston in Sandwick is a large house called Doehouse. The owner found one day that a large sum of money, five pounds, had been stolen. He ordered a young servant to take his horse and to ride to Sati's house and tell him to come tomorrow morning to solve the crime. As the farmer didn't want his business being known he instructed the boy that on no account was he to get off his horse, just deliver the message and then leave as quickly as possible. He set off, riding hard, until he arrived at Sati's house. The bare hillside provided no cover and so his approach was observed and Sati slipped into his hiding place. His wife went outside to greet the boy, but he refused to go inside, saying, 'Tell Sati that his service is wanted at Doehouse tomorrow morning.'

Sati's wife tried to grab the reins, but the boy turned his horse and galloped off down the hillside. Sati was in a right fix; he had absolutely no information to work on. If he got it wrong then his reputation was lost, but if he didn't go then his reputation was also ruined. He had a sleepless night, but set off at first light on the long walk to Doehouse. When he arrived the farmer instructed him to go to the kitchen for something to eat, which he gladly did. It was only then that the farmer muttered to him, 'I've had some money stolen, but I don't want people to know about it. The ranzelman[45] has drawn a blank but I'm damned if I can afford to lose such a large sum of money. Five pounds was taken, so you can see why I'm keen to get it back.'

'Why, yes indeed,' said Sati, munching his way through a bere bannock and cheese.

Sati's eye fell on an iron cooking pot and an idea started to form in his cunning mind. Once he had eaten his fill he said that he was ready to reveal the culprit.

'Now then,' he said to the farmer, 'I want the biggest cooking pot that you have and a live black cock. Then I want everyone to gather in the hall and the thief shall be revealed.'

The farmer did as he was told and everyone gathered together in the hall. Sati turned the cooking pot upside down and put the cock underneath it. Then he issued his orders.

'Now everyone in this room, starting with the farmer and his wife, for no one is above suspicion, will do as you see me do now.'

Sati walked three times around the pot, against the course of the sun, as all evil-doers conduct their business, then he laid his hands on the bottom of the cooking pot and, spreading his fingers wide, he raised them in front of himself.

'I want you all to do exactly as I have done and when the guilty party touches the pot then the cock will crow.'

First the farmer did it, then his wife and the rest of his family, but the cock remained silent. As each person raised their hands Sati checked them to see if they were sooty from the bottom of the cooking pot; so that he knew that they had indeed touched it.

Then the servants did it, in order of their importance within the household, but still the cock remained quiet while all their hands were sooty. It was just the farm labourers left, and the sweat was starting to break out on Sati's brow. His reputation was all he had and if that was lost then he would starve. At last a young man who hadn't been at the farm for very long stepped forward. He looked shaken and nervous as he walked three times around the pot and then put his hands to the pot, but when he raised them there was no sign of any soot on them.

'You didn't touch the pot,' said Sati, 'why is that?'

The man looked like he was about to faint.

'Here is your thief,' declared Sati.

The young man confessed on the spot that it was indeed he who stole the money. He was escorted to the hiding place where he had stashed the money and it was returned to the farmer. Sati received a handsome reward for solving the case and he returned home with his reputation intact. You see, Sati might not have known magic, but the one thing that he did know was human nature!

10

GHOSTS

⊱ THE BLACK WIFE OF SCAR ⊰
AND HER SISTERS

John Traill was the laird of Westove in Sanday and he lived at Scar House in the early 1800s. He had made money in India, serving in the army, and while he was out there he took an Indian woman as his wife. They had four daughters together and everything went well until a letter arrived to say that his father was seriously ill and not expected to live long. This meant that he would inherit the estate and must return to Orkney as soon as possible. He made arrangements for his daughters' education, leaving them in the care of a friend with sufficient funds to see that they were well provided for. He then prepared to leave, but so did his wife. He asked her coldly why she was packing as he had no intention of bringing her to Orkney with him. It was fine to have a black wife in India, but not so in the circles in which he moved in his native land. His wife's dark eyes smouldered and she said, 'I will be at Scar with you; living or dead.'

He took a ship back to England and everything went well for the first part of the journey. But little did he know that his Indian wife had stowed away aboard the ship and was watching him. One night, as he stood by the rail of the ship looking at the vast

darkness of the ocean, his wife slipped silently by his side and said, 'I told you that I'd be at Scar with you, living or dead.'

Traill was stunned by the sight of her standing beside him on the deck of the ship. He looked around and saw that there was no one to be seen so he grabbed his wife and threw her over the side of the ship. As he did that a seagull flew past and cried its screeching cry. Ever after that he could not stand to hear the cry of a seagull. The blood raced through his veins and beat in his ears as he stood there, the enormity of his crime starting to dawn on him. But no one had seen her on board and no one had seen her murdered, so he was free to carry on his life as he saw fit.

He returned to Sanday and took up residence in Scar House; a large, rambling building that had been built in three stages over a period of time. It lies by the sea, where the seagulls constantly fly. His Indian wife and family were never mentioned and he was free to look for a new wife who would bring with her a dowry and maybe some more land.

One winter's night a servant girl went to the byre to milk the cows. Her only light was a flickering flame from the old cruisie lamp that burned fish oil with a rush wick. As she was milking the flame went out, leaving her in darkness. She thought that the cow must have flicked it with her tail, when suddenly the flame returned. This was very strange, but the girl continued milking. Then the light went out again only to return after a few seconds. The girl looked towards the lamp and her blood ran cold as she saw a black hand reaching out towards the flame and lifting it from the wick. After playing with it for a few seconds the hand returned the flame to its rightful place. The black wife of Scar had kept her word by saying that she would be there; living or dead.

The haunting was not just confined to the byre for one of the rooms in the middle section of the house always had strange sounds emitting from it and strange, unexplainable events happening. It became known as 'Peggy's Hole'; though why it was 'Peggy's' in particular is unknown.

John Traill died of what was termed 'not a very good disease', which was the polite way of referring to syphilis. In his latter days he was unable to walk, so they used to sit him in a chair outside in the garden where he could feel the sun on his face. It was a pale sun compared to the one that once shone on him in Madras. But day after day he sat there, being constantly tormented by the sound that reminded him of his crime. He died in his chair as the seagulls cried in the skies above him.

This is not the only 'black wife' story from Orkney, which makes me wonder if this is a type of story that is found in other areas.

Old Nisthouse, Harray, was once the home of the Clouston family who were said to have had an interest in the slave trade. It was said that one of them brought home a black woman who lived with him for a time before disappearing. After that a black shape, known as the 'black wife' was seen in the field behind the house. A friend of mine's mother saw it when she was a little girl, around 1900, and described it as a shapeless black mist rising up from the ground.

The other haunting is at the house of Melsetter in North Walls on the island of Hoy. It was owned for a long time by the Moodie family. Captain James Moodie, of the Royal Navy, was fatally shot in Broad Street, Kirkwall, in 1725 as part of a feud. It is said that his ghost still walks the grounds of Melsetter House. But he has company, it seems. The Moodies sold the estate to the Heddle family in the early part of the nineteenth century. They adopted the name Moodie-Heddle through marriage and had business interests in Africa, including, it was said, slavery. One of the Moodie-Heddles returned to Orkney with a beautiful black woman, who lived with him for a time before disappearing. It was said that her ghost was seen in one of the rooms of the old house (since rebuilt) and walking in the grounds of the house. On another occasion a maid went into the nursery to put fuel on the fire and saw a woman standing in front of the fire, her arms resting on the mantelpiece and she was sobbing. The maid asked her what was wrong and the stranger turned around, revealing herself to be a black woman. The maid knew of the ghost and fled the room as quickly as she could.

⸱◌⸱ THE PHANTOM HAND ◌⸱

The Links of Warsetter in Sanday is a large stretch of sandy ground that slopes down towards the sea. Large numbers of grey seals gather together to bask on the white, sandy beach that lies at its foot; a place where people seldom go.

Where you get these sandy links you also get rabbits as the soft, well-drained ground is ideal for them. Once upon a time it was illegal to poach rabbits, as they were used by the big house as a source of meat. On the Links of Warsetter used to stand a house called Grindley, now long since gone. One night, under the cover of darkness, the man of Grindley set off to check his rabbit snares,

to see if he would get a dinner out of them. He saw that one rabbit had gone down a rabbit hole with his snare, so he put his hand down the hole to retrieve it. Suddenly, a cold hand gripped his one and a thin voice said:

> Thoo can haad an' I'll draa,
> Till the cock o' Grindley does craa.[46]

The phantom hand had him in a vice-like grip and there was nothing that he could do but to wait there all night until the cock of Grindley crowed in the morning, at which moment the ghostly hand disappeared and the man was released from its grasp.

⸙ THE WHITE LADY OF CLESTRAIN ⸙

The Hall of Clestrain in Orphir was the birthplace of the Arctic explorer, Dr John Rae (1813–93), who mapped over 1,750 miles of the coast of Arctic Canada. The house in which he lived was a replacement for a much earlier house, which still lies down by the sea and was used as a storehouse in Rae's day. As a boy he knew the following story and said that he would often see ghostly, flickering lights emanating from the house at night, which made his blood freeze with terror. He later discovered that these lights were caused by smugglers signalling to a boat at sea that the coast was clear for landing gin and brandy.

In the mid-eighteenth century the laird of Clestrain was William Honyman, a great, blustering bully of a man, quick to anger and handy with his fists. Despite his signing a 'Declaration for the Suppression of Smuggling' it was said that there was no greater offender than him. Estate tenants paid their rent in kind, with grain being the main form of exchange. This grain was much in demand in areas like the Hebrides and Norway, where the lairds would buy goods to bring back to Orkney and sell here. In 1758 Honyman decided that his son, Mungo, should join him on his latest trip down to the Hebrides with a boatload of grain to sell. His wife, Mary, was against the idea of her young son going on such a dangerous voyage, but William had made up his mind and once that was made up then he could not be persuaded otherwise. No matter how much she begged and wept he remained resolute and said that it was time for the boy to learn the trade of buying and selling.

William Honyman had a personal servant called John, a man cut from the same cloth as his master. The boat was prepared and made ready for the sea voyage that lay ahead of it and the grain was put into sacks ready to be loaded on board once they were ready to sail. Before they left, Honyman took a large wooden box and filled it with his valuables. Rumour had it that it contained a large sum of money, family jewellery and a bag of Spanish dollars. He and his servant, John, carried the box up to the old hill dyke that separated the arable land from the common grazing on the hills above. They buried the box and on his return he instructed his wife to keep a watch on the hill dyke. The cargo was loaded and the laird set sail with his son and his servant, John, as crew. The heavily laden boat

sailed across the bay, out through the Hoy Sound into the Atlantic Ocean and disappeared from view.

Three months passed without news and then one evening in late August the laird's boat was seen coming in through Hoy Sound and towards Clestrain. Mary and the servants gathered on the shore in eager anticipation of unloading the cargo that they had bought in the Hebrides. As the boat drew nearer they could see two figures standing in the bow of the boat and the laird at the helm. The boat sped swiftly towards its usual anchorage but when it reached the spot it slowly dissolved into thin air and was gone. The shock of seeing this phantom ship was too much for Mary's sensitive nature and she had to be helped back to the house, where she died soon afterwards. News finally came which told how the laird, his son and servant were lost off Cape Wrath on their first day out of Orkney when the overloaded boat was swamped by a heavy sea.

It was often said that the figure of a lady in white could be seen floating along the old hill dyke in the evening's dying light. Mary Honyman still guards the treasure that her husband entrusted her with. It was also said that on the anniversary of his death, the ghost of the laird and his servant can be seen down by the shore preparing the cargo and getting ready to sail.

Strangely enough, another house associated with Dr John Rae has a ghost story attached to it. After Dr Rae retired he and his wife lived at Berstane House, to the east of Kirkwall. My mother once told me of a story that she heard of a girl who was a servant in the house; after Rae's time. The girl had become pregnant but had managed to conceal the fact from her employer, as she feared that she would be dismissed if he found out. One night she went into labour alone in her bedroom. They found her in the morning; she had passed out after the birth from the shock, pain and exhaustion and the baby had suffocated under the blankets. What happened to the girl, I don't know, but it was said that her ghost still walks the corridors of the house, searching for her lost child.

THE GHOST OF KIRKHOUSE

There was once a dairymaid who worked at Kirkhouse in South Ronaldsay. She was said to be a notorious liar and she would often claim that she saw ghosts in the local kirkyard. When people said that they didn't believe her she would reply, 'May my feet go rotten and drop off if it isn't true!'

Strange to say, she fell victim to a disease that caused her feet to go gangrenous and they had to be amputated before she died. It is said that her ghost can be seen walking down a passage, holding a foot under each arm.

⸎ THE WATCH ᔐ

Peter Mowat from Rackwick in Hoy had been visiting Longhope on business and was returning home along the cliffs. When he reached a place called the Geo Heads he met two strangers who were dressed in seamen's clothing. The one stepped forward and asked him if he had the time on him. Peter took out his pocketwatch and told the man what the time was. The stranger looked at the watch in Peter's hand and said, 'Where did you get that watch?'

'I bought it in Wick when I was there at the fishing,' said Peter.

'If you open the back of that watch,' said the stranger, 'you will find the number 33707 engraved on the inside of the back casing.'

'Why, there might be indeed,' said Peter, 'in truth I have never looked, but I will now.'

He opened the back of the watch and sure enough the number was there.

'How did you know that number was there?' asked Peter.

'It is my watch,' replied the stranger, 'my corpse lies at the foot of this geo and the watch was stolen from me by a man from Longhope. There is a gold chain that goes with it too, which is still in my pocket, but the Longhope man became too scared to recover it.

He sold the watch in Wick. You bought it in good faith, not knowing its history, but I have something to ask you to do for me. Take a boat and recover my body and give me a Christian burial. You can have the gold chain as your payment. Do this for me and you will never want for as long as you live but, if you refuse to do it, you will have no rest by day or night.'

With that the two men disappeared into thin air. Peter ran home, as fast as his feet would carry him. He was afraid to carry out the ghost's wishes, but still he was more afraid of what would happen if he didn't, so he gathered a crew of elderly men and set off towards the geo. He found the fisherman's skeleton just where he said it would be; lying on a ledge of rock above the sea. He recognised the clothing as that worn by the man that he had met on the clifftop, but it was ragged and tattered from exposure to the elements. Inside the waistcoat pocket he found the gold chain and clipped it onto his watch. The man's remains were taken aboard the boat and brought to Rackwick and a funeral was arranged right away.

⁄ The Unbaptised Bairn's Ghost ⁄

It was once believed that if a baby died without being baptised then it couldn't rest as it wasn't allowed to enter heaven without a name. Walter Traill Dennison recalled being asked by an illiterate couple to write the name of a stillborn baby on a slip of paper so that they could pin it onto the shroud to act as a 'passport to paradise'. This was in the 1840s, so imagine my surprise to hear of it being done in my family in 1912. My great-uncle, Johnny Ernest Trousdell Drever, was married and his wife was expecting a baby. He had a job carting goods for a shop and was living at his wife's parents' house at the time. Before he left the house one morning he told his wife, Maggie, not to go to work in the kelp as she was nearly at her full term and the work was too heavy for her. After he left, his wife's father made her go to the shore and carry up the heavy wet kelp with the others, which led to her miscarrying the baby boy that she was carrying. Johnny wrote the name 'George Drever' on a slip of paper and pinned it to the shroud; he also had a gravestone erected bearing the child's name, which can still be seen in the Pierowall cemetery in Westray to this day. Sadly, they had no more children.

In the farm of Mirland in Deerness there is a mound called Howedooack. It was said that a servant girl on the farm had an illegitimate baby that she killed as soon as it was born, burying the body in the mound. After that the ghost of a bairn was heard crying around the mound and it would follow people walking along the rough road that ran close by it. At that time there was a pub at Smiddybanks where ale could be bought (it closed in the 1880s). One night a man was heading home from the pub with a full head of steam when he heard the sound of a bairn coming crying behind him. He suffered it for a while before losing his temper and saying, 'Hadd awey wae thee, bare erse!'[47]

As soon as he said 'bare erse' the crying stopped, for the child had been given a name.

My grandmother, Davina Drever, told the story of a child's ghost who haunted a road in Westray. In the 1890s she was walking home from school with a friend when a white light rose from the road and floated in front of them. Many people saw it at various times until a minister went and spoke to it, after which it was never seen again.

✍ THE WHITE HORSE OF CLUMLY ୭৲

At the end of the nineteenth century there were two young men working as labourers at the farm of Clumly in Sandwick. Everything was going fine until a pretty young girl from a neighbouring parish came to work there. Her beauty captivated both the young men and they started to court her. Flattered by the attention, the girl was happy to lead them on, not favouring the one above the other. Soon tempers started to fray as the two men tried to win the heart of the girl; any thoughts of a former friendship were dispelled and a bitter hatred took hold within them. It all came to a tragic conclusion one night when these two rivals were sent to the barn to thresh sheaves of corn. Facing each other with their flails in their hands they started to argue over the girl. Soon the insults were flying and their blood got hot. One of the men took up his flail and struck his rival over the head with it, killing him instantly. Faced with the sudden realisation of what he had done the murderer knew that he had to dispose of the body or face the hangman's rope. He dragged the dead body over to the corner of the barn and piled straw over it to hide it from view. Once darkness fell he took a white horse from the farm and, putting the body into a sack, threw it over the horse's back. He rode the horse as fast as he could towards the cliffs of Yesnaby, which stand tall and dark against the might of the Atlantic Ocean. He heard the sound of the waves far below, pounding against the cliff-face and it was into that churning sea that he threw his victim's body. Mounting once more he rode back to the farm as fast as he could. As they neared the farm he urged the horse on to gallop towards a drystone dyke that surrounded one of the fields. He tried to get the horse to jump it, but its back hooves clipped the top of the wall, tearing down the top row of stones as it did so, before falling heavily to the ground. Both the horse and the rider were killed by the fall and their bodies were found lying there the next day. No matter how often people tried to rebuild the top row of stones on that dyke they are always on the ground once more the following morning. It is said that the ghost of the white horse and its rider can be seen in the evening, racing towards the cliffs at Yesnaby, forever condemned to relive that fateful night until the end of time.

⚬ THE STOLEN WINDING SHEET ⚬

The following story took place in the Cross parish of Sanday. Babbie Skethaway was dying, and she knew it. All her life she had been very particular about everything and her death was to be no exception. She called the local howdy wife, Black Jock, to her house to discuss arrangements. The howdy wife was a midwife, district nurse and undertaker, all rolled into one. Black Jock was a rough woman with very little feminine charms and was so like her father in appearance and nature that everyone called her by his name. Babbie told her how she wanted her funeral to be and she pointed towards the large chest of drawers, telling Black Jock to look in the bottom drawer for her winding sheet; the shroud that she was to be buried in. Black Jock took out the garment and looked at it; it was beautiful, made from the finest silk and richly embroidered.

'Do you think that it will fit me?' asked Babbie. 'Or should I try it on?'

'No, no; I can see fine that it will fit you,' said Black Jock.

Soon poor old Babbie passed away and Black Jock washed her body and dressed her in her fine winding sheet ready for her final journey. At the funeral the drink flowed freely, for Babbie had made arrangements so that nothing was wanting. Black Jock drank like a beast, and as she grew more intoxicated so the more she hovered over Babbie's open coffin, fingering the silken shroud and muttering to herself, 'What a waste to put such a fine garment into the earth. What a waste; what a waste!'

Babbie's coffin was carried to the Cross kirk and she was buried in the kirkyard there. Back at Babbie's house afterwards, more drink flowed and Black Jock drank her fill.

Later that night, fuelled with home-made whisky and greed, Black Jock took a spade and set off under cover of darkness to the Cross kirkyard. She dug up Babbie's grave and tore the silken winding sheet from her poor, wizened body, leaving her in her grave as naked as she had been when she had come into the world. She hurriedly filled in the grave and returned home with the stolen winding sheet, which she hid in the bottom of a big kist[48] in her house.

Not long after this horrible event a man called Andrew Moodie was walking home late one night. He had been sent on an errand by his master and, to his horror, he found that his way home led him past the Cross kirkyard and the sun was already setting. As it grew darker a terrible storm started to brew, with blue sheets of lightning tearing the black sky. It seemed to Andrew that the darkest piece of sky was right over the top of the Cross kirkyard, and a feeling of dread took a hold of him. As he drew nearer to the burial ground the wind rose and the rain lashed down so hard that he was blinded by it. But if that was bad it was nothing compared to the sight that next met his eyes, for as he approached the kirkyard gate he saw something which he never quite recovered from. Great pillars of coloured light, as tall as a ship's mast, rose up from every grave, swaying slightly and burning like fire. The pillars were blue, yellow, green and red in colour, sometimes they changed so that it was impossible to say what colour they were. On top of each of these pillars of light stood the ghosts of the people who had been buried in the graves below. Some had only one ghost, others two, three or four ghosts, depending on the number who were buried there. They were of every age from old people to young babies and they were all talking together in voices that made Andrew's blood run as cold as ice. He couldn't understand the language of the dead, and he didn't want to know what they were saying either. Among their number was one poor ghost who stood there naked. The other ghosts pointed towards her and shook their heads. Some pitied her, others mocked her, for the dead retain all the vices and nature of their living selves. Andrew recognised the naked ghost as Babbie Skethaway and he saw her staring around her, searching for something. Then, to Andrew's horror, her head started to turn towards him. He knew that the look from a ghost is enough to break a man's mind and he didn't wait for Babbie's gaze to fix on him; he turned and fled the scene. But the ghosts saw him and each one rose from their pillar of light, flew up into the air and began to chase him down the road. He ran like all the devils in hell were after him until he arrived at the nearest house, which happened to be Bea; Black Jock's home.

Andrew battered on the door and begged to be let in. After what seemed to be a lifetime to Andrew the door opened and Black Jock grabbed him and pulled him over the threshold before slamming the door shut. He saw that every hole in the house had been barricaded and protected with steel. Knives, awls, pins and a sickle were driven into the wooden barricades as a protection against evil spirits. Her cat sat quivering in the corner of the room, ears flattened against its head with fear. Black Jock's husband was away for the night, so she was on her own. Her poor husband was a witless man who was bullied relentlessly by his wife. As a result he took every opportunity to go visiting people and then staying so late that they offered for him to stay the night. People felt sorry for him and so endured his company as an act of kindness.

Andrew tried to tell Black Jock what he had seen, but she threw a peat at him, hitting him on the knee which made him cry with pain. Black Jock sat by the fire. She had drawn a circle around herself with a steel pin, which she held in her hand, muttering spells all the time. Suddenly the ghosts were upon them. They broke against the walls like a wave of malice, crying and roaring in their unearthly tongue. One ghost pulled the blocking from the hole in the flagstone roof above the door that the cat used as a door to get in and out of the house. However, as it did so it touched the steel blade of the sickle that was sticking there and it gave a loud cry of pain. This seemed to frighten the other ghosts as they all fled from the house. Then they grew angry and, returning, attacked the house with all their might. They went around the house, over the house and even underneath the house, roaring with rage as they went. Black Jock held her steel pin tightly in her grasp and muttered the spells that would protect her within the circle that she had drawn on the floor.

Andrew lay crouched on the floor under a window, cowering with fear. Suddenly, the barricade over the window was torn away and what should he see but Babbie Skethaway's ghostly head and long neck stretching in through the opening and moaning, 'Where's my sheet? Where's my winding sheet? It's cold, cold to lie in the ground, mother naked. Give me back my sheet!'

Her long, bony arms were now thrust through the window opening and they waved to and fro, grasping the air as they went. One of her hands struck Andrew on the top of the head, knocking him unconscious. It was said that not a hair grew on his head where Babbie's three fingers struck him. He collapsed on the floor, and one of his feet struck Black Jock's hand, knocking the steel pin from her grasp. Without the protection of steel Black Jock was now vulnerable, so she ran to the kist and opened the lid. The stolen winding sheet leapt up into the air in a blue flame and flew straight towards Babbie's ghost.

'Take back your damned winding sheet, and my curse with it!' cried Black Jock.

A ghost struck Black Jock on the back and pushed her face first to the floor. Before they could exact any more revenge upon her

the sun rose and the cock crowed. The ghosts rose from the ground and flew back to their graves, like a colony of bats returning to their cave.

When her neighbours arrived at the scene Black Jock's house was little more than a ruin. All the cattle that were tied in the byre were lying dead on the floor. Andrew was senseless and took a while to recover from the ordeal. But Black Jock remained fixed to the floor and no matter how many people pulled at her they could not move her. The ghosts had fixed her to the spot and it took magic and forespoken[49] water to break the spell. The charms used to make this form of remedy were kept secret, especially from the minister. Black Jock did recover, but you can be sure that she avoided the Cross kirkyard after dark and she never dug up another grave for as long as she lived!

⁓ JARL SIGURD THE STOUT'S GHOST ARMY ⁓

Jarl[50] Sigurd the Stout ruled Orkney from 995–1014 and was the last of the pagan jarls. Not long after he took over the rule of the islands he was threatened by a superior army of Scots who wanted to control the north of what is now Scotland. Sigurd had an Irish mother called Eithne, who had a reputation for sorcery and witchcraft, and he asked her for her help in winning the battle. She looked at him scornfully, saying, 'Had I known that you wanted to live forever I'd have reared you in my wool basket.'

Sigurd's blood boiled inside of him, but he held his tongue. His mother took a banner and handed it to him, saying, 'I have made this banner with all the skill that I possess but it has this doom woven into it. It will bring victory to the army that carries it before them but death to the standard bearer who holds it.'

The banner depicted a raven in flight and it looked as if it was flying in the air above them when they raised it. The raven was Odin's bird and the life of the standard bearer was a sacrifice to him. It proved successful in bringing victory to Sigurd in that battle, but at the loss of three standard bearers.

In 1014 Sigurd took an army from Orkney to fight alongside Sygtrygg Silk-Beard at Contarf in Ireland. Before he left Orkney, his faithful servant, Harek, asked to join him in the battle, but Sigurd refused his request as he thought that he was too old. To soften the blow Sigurd

promised him that he would be the first
to hear the outcome of the battle. The
battle was long and hard but Sigurd's
men held their position in the centre of
the army.

During the battle a man in Caithness saw a group
of twelve women riding to a weaving hut and go inside.
He peeped through the window and the sight that he
saw made his blood run cold, for these were no ordinary
women but the Valkyries; the handmaidens of Odin
and the choosers of the slain. They set up a loom and
started to weave the web of war, directing the course of
the battle. The uprights of the loom were made of spears
and they wove a web made from human entrails, using
arrows as shuttles and swords as weaving batons while
human heads served as loom weights. They sang as they
wove until the fate of the battle was decided, when they
tore the web to pieces, each one taking a part.

In Ireland Jarl Sigurd's line was broken and three
standard bearers had been killed. He ordered another man to take
up the banner, but the man replied, 'Bear your own devil, Jarl.'

Sigurd tore the banner from its pole, wrapped it up and thrust it
underneath his cloak. Just as he had done that he was run through
with a spear and was killed.

Harek waited at home for news of his master. One day he saw
the jarl riding up with some of his men on horseback. Harek took
a horse and rode out to meet him. People saw him stop and talk to
Jarl Sigurd for a short while. Then they all turned their horses and
Harek followed them behind a hill and out of sight. Harek and Jarl
Sigurd the Stout's ghostly army were never seen again.

11

SHIPWRECKS

 TALES OF THE SPANISH ARMADA

In 1588 the Spanish Armada was driven north by the wind and scattered around the coast of Scotland and Ireland. One ship was lost on Fair Isle in Shetland, but despite tales of the Armada in Orkney there are no recorded wrecks. These low-lying islands have claimed many vessels over the years, however, and it would actually be strange if there weren't any Armada wrecks amongst them. One thing that there is plenty of in Orkney is tales of the Spanish Armada.

One of these tales is of a ship that foundered off North Ronaldsay. The crew took to the ship's boat and headed towards this island. However, on approaching the coast they saw dark shapes huddled among the rocks on the shore and, thinking that it was men waiting in ambush, they turned their boat away. In fact, what they had seen was the ancient breed of North Ronaldsay sheep that eats seaweed and lives on the shore of the island.

Another boatload of Spanish sailors arrived in the sheltered harbour of Pierowall in Westray and they were made welcome by the local people. Scotland was an independent country in those days and the Spanish were seen as nothing more than shipwrecked sailors in need of help and not as an enemy. These Spanish sailors married local girls and settled down. They were always called the Dons and many Westray families were said to be descended from them. Once these Dons had settled and started to raise families of their own they made a pact that no Don should marry outside of another Don family. This went on for some time before a young Don man fell in love with a Westray girl who had no Spanish blood in her. They courted in secret, as the other Dons would never allow them to be together. The young man went to the minister and asked if he could read their banns at the kirk three times that Sunday and then marry them, in order to prevent the Dons from stopping the wedding. This was agreed and the banns were read three times and the happy couple were wed. That night, as the young Don held his new bride in his arms, the other Dons arrived and pulled him from his marriage bed. He was roughly taken outside and received such a savage beating that he was hardly able to crawl back to his bed, where he died soon after.

I remember being told a story from my own family, not about my brown-eyed and dark-haired mother's side from Westray, but about my father's side. The story went that a Spanish Armada ship was wrecked off Start Point in Sanday and one of the survivors was a dark-skinned Moor from North Africa; possible a galley slave. He settled on Sanday and started a family, which was where my family name of Muir came from.

Walter Traill Dennison from Sanday had a sword in his private antiquarian collection at his home of West Brough that was said to have come from an officer of the Spanish Armada who died in the house of a Mr Traill (although we do not know which Traill this was). It was said that the officer thanked Traill for his kindness and offered him his sword as the only thing of value that he had left.

The officer was said to have been buried in St Magnus Cathedral, but there is no historical evidence for this tale and no Armada burials in the cathedral.

George Marwick (1836–1912) had many tales about an Armada ship that was smashed against the rocks at his native Yesnaby in the West Mainland. The survivors were also called 'The Dons', said to be from local people overhearing them refer to one or more of their number as 'don'. A local man, who went to see what could be gleaned from the wreck, found a priest lying on the ground, near death. He held in his hand a large silver cross, which he was staring at with a fixed gaze. The local man gave him a stroke on the head with a staff, killing the priest, before stealing the cross. Some of the survivors saw this act of barbarity and gave chase. Eventually the offender took refuge in a church where the minister acted as mediator.

It was eventually agreed that the cross could remain at the little kirk where it had been carried.

One of the survivors walked a few miles down the coast before finding shelter under an earth dyke in the district of Outertown, Stromness. When the local people found him there, nearly dead from exposure, they took pity on him and gave him shelter and warm food. He was later allowed to build a home for himself; the site of his house is still called 'The Don' to this day.

An infamous doctor called Tallian lived in Stromness and was said to be descended from a medical doctor on the Armada ship. He used to dig up dead bodies to remove the fat from around the heart, which was said to be a cure against certain diseases. He built a house which is still called 'Wheeldon' (spelt Quildon) to this day; meaning 'quoy' (enclosure) 'don'. 'Qu' was pronounced 'wh' in olden times.

Other survivors were said to have started families, of which there are more stories. One interesting tale is of a Spanish survivor called Sebastian. He married a local woman and they had a son, who was named after his father. The local children, who still spoke the old Norn language, found the name 'Sebastian' difficult to pronounce and could only say 'Sabiston', which is a surname still in use in the West Mainland.

✎ CHARLIE'S HOLE ✎

On Wednesday, 5 March 1834, the inhabitants of Outertown in Stromness saw a ship being driven by a storm towards the high cliffs called the Black Craig. The Dundee-registered ship was called the *Star* and was sailing to Wick from Bristol. On board the ship the crew could do nothing to save themselves as the huge seas pounded their vessel.

The local folk gathered at the top of the Black Craig with simmans; ropes made from twisted straw. As the ship was pushed right up against the side of the cliff they lowered their ropes to the crew that they could see on the deck below them. Suddenly, a huge wave rolled in from the Atlantic and broke against the ship with such ferocity that the vessel was smashed to pieces in an instant. The people found themselves helpless witnesses to a tragedy that they were powerless to do anything about. The ship was gone and there was no sign of the crew in the boiling water below. With heavy hearts they returned home to their firesides as the storm raged outside. And rage it did, for several days without a break, the wind howled and the seas pounded the cliffs and the shores.

The following Sunday the winds dropped and the people could once again go about as normal. Then a stranger arrived at a house near to the Black Craig, much to the surprise of the owners. He said that his name was Charlie and that he was from the ship that had been wrecked four days previously. The people could hardly believe that anyone could have survived that wreck, let along stay alive for days. He then told them of his miraculous escape. At the foot of the Black Craig there is a large sea cave, carved deep into the rock by the pounding of the Atlantic waves. When the ship was smashed by the wave he was washed into this cave. Normally he would have been killed by the force of the waves entering the cave, but luckily part of the broken hull of the ship was driven against the mouth of the cave and this acted as a breakwater. He found that there was a raised beach at the back of the cave where he could get away from the sea. He was also lucky enough to find a barrel of ship's biscuits and some salted fish that had washed inside the

cave as well, so he had some food. He also had a supply of fresh water as it trickled through the fissures in the rock in the roof of the cave. He settled down and waited until the storm finally died down and he could try to escape. Once it had done so he tried to leave the cave, but found that the only way out was to climb up the high cliffs of the Black Craig, which he managed to do and reached the top. He then headed for the first house he saw and safety. To this day the spectacular cave at the foot of the Black Craig is called 'Charlie's Hole'.

The Wreck of the *Pennsylvania*

The SS *Pennsylvania* was wrecked on the island of Swona on Monday, 27 July 1931. The ship was sailing from New York to Copenhagen with a rich cargo, including large quantities of cigarettes, typewriters and even Cadillac cars. It had encountered fog not long after leaving port and remained shrouded by it all the way across the Atlantic. The captain had been on the bridge for ninety-three hours without sleep before his ship struck the rocks. At first he refused the assistance of the Longhope lifeboat, but after a day the crew were forced to take to the ship's boats and abandon her. At that time it was seen as no crime to take what you could from a wreck before the sea claimed it. Many islanders were skilled at stripping wrecks, but the real professionals were the men of Stroma; the island that lies in the middle of the Pentland Firth and is part of the county of Caithness. It was said that the Stroma men could smell a wreck. The John o' Groats men also had a reputation for being great 'wreckers' too. No one lured ships onto rocks (which is the stuff of fiction), but if a ship struck then they were not slow to help themselves.

The *Pennsylvania* remained above the water for a week before its back was broken and it disappeared under the waves forever.

The customs officers were keen to get aboard the ship and make an inventory of the cargo, but legend has it that the local boat owners were as keen to prevent them from doing so. Many excuses were found that prevented them from taking the officials to the wreck and they were left on the shore, watching the wreck like hawks.

One night, under the cover of the summer twilight, a boat from South Ronaldsay set off for the wreck. The men on board couldn't show a light, as this would alert the customs officers to their illegal salvage expedition. The ship, by this time, was not in good shape and the men knew that she could break up at any moment and so speed was necessary if they wanted to win their prize and escape with their lives. They boarded the ship and headed to the hold where they grabbed the first two boxes that they could get their hands on without stopping to see what they contained. Hurriedly, they got the boxes into their boat and set off back to the shore with them. The boxes were then transferred to a hiding place where they could be opened and the contents shared out between the hopeful men. Imagine their shock and disappointment when they saw what was inside the boxes; the very same boxes that they had risked their lives to obtain. One box contained shrouds for dead bodies and the other contained condoms! One old South Ronaldsay man told me the fate of the condoms, 'The bairns used them for balloons,' he said, with a mischievous chuckle.

✎ FATED TO DROWN ✎

The following story was written by the Reverend James Wallace, minister of St Magnus Cathedral, and published in 1693 after his death. This gives you an idea of the age of the tale.

There was a man by the name of John Smith who lived on the island of Stronsay. He and three neighbours used to rise at dawn and take a small boat out fishing around the island waters. After they had been going to the sea for several days on end, and had a good supply of fish, John Smith's wife asked him not to go out the following day, as he was worn out and needed to rest. He said that he couldn't let his neighbours down and that he would have to go. She wasn't happy about this and decided to take matters into her own hands. That night, as her husband slept, she covered up what windows they had in their house and stopped up any holes that let in light until the room was as dark as pitch. He remained asleep, exhausted by the work that he had been doing. Having done this his wife went out to work in the fields, happy in the knowledge that her husband would get a well-deserved rest.

The neighbours gathered together by the boat and got it ready to go fishing. John Smith didn't turn up, so they left without him and set sail to go to their fishing grounds. No one knows what happened that day, but their boat capsized and all the men were drowned. News soon reached home that the boat was lost and the men's lives were ended. Mrs Smith heard the sorry news as she worked in the fields. She was shocked and saddened by the event, but within her heart she was also glad that she had saved her husband's life by preventing him from going to the fishing that day. She ran home to tell him the news, but on entering their home she made a terrible discovery, for her husband lay dead on the floor. He had got up in the total darkness of the room and had tripped up, falling with his head inside the 'strang tub' where they collected urine that was used for shrinking homemade cloth. It was his doom to drown that day and no matter how hard you try, you cannot escape your own fate!

ᘒ Archie Angel ᘒ

One stormy day in the early 1730s a woman of Seaquoy at Aikerness in Westray, whose surname was Rendall, sat by her fire spinning wool as the wind howled around the house like an animal in torment. Suddenly the door opened and her husband came in, saying, 'There's a big three-masted ship heading towards the rocks at the Arches of Rammigeo. I'm going next door to get Jock of Wheelingstanes to see if we can help the men on board.'

'Well, take care,' said his wife, 'for it's not a night to be out in that weather.'

He assured her that he would be all right and left the house as his wife muttered a silent prayer for the lives of those on board the doomed ship.

When the two men reached the shore there were already many men gathered there, watching the ship as it drew nearer. Its sails were torn and it was utterly helpless at the mercy of the wind and the tide. On board the crew where running around in a panic, trying desperately to save their ship and their own lives. Among them was a woman; no one knows who she was although some thought that she might have been the captain's wife. The woman had a child, a little boy, no more than a toddler. She wrapped her shawl around him and tied him close to her breast. Just before the ship struck the rocks she leapt overboard, clutching her son tightly as she entered the wild, raging sea. At that moment the ship struck the rocks and the bottom was torn out of it. The ship quickly went to pieces, too far from the shore for anyone to help the unfortunate crew. Seeing that there was nothing that they could do the men returned to their homes for the night.

The next morning, as soon as it was light, the men returned to the shore to see what they could salvage from the wreck. In a treeless island like Westray wood was a valuable commodity and nothing was wasted. One man's misfortune was good luck to another and a rich bounty from the sea could be the difference between life and death for an old person or a sickly child during a hard winter. The men gathered up pieces of timber, ropes, sail cloth, barrels and whatever cargo the ship was carrying that had washed ashore. Every now and then they would come across a body lying on the shore and they would drag it up to the land to receive a decent burial later. As the Rendall man of Seaquoy walked along the beach he came across the body of a woman lying dead. He looked at her with sadness and thought to himself, 'It's a terrible thing, the sea.'

Then he saw that the woman had a small child tied to her and a lump came to his throat at the sight of this tragedy. He then noticed that the child made a slight movement and gave a little cry; it was alive! He untied the child from his dead mother and ran home with him to his wife. She stripped the boy and dried him, wrapping him in blankets by the fire and warmed some milk to give him. If the boy could speak any words at all then it was nothing that the folk of Westray understood. He soon grew in strength and recovered totally from his ordeal. He remained with the Rendall family at Seaquoy and was brought up as one of their own.

No one knew anything about the ship that was lost; the only clue was a piece of wood with writing on it, which the man of Seaquoy had found. He couldn't read, so he took it to the minister who looked at it and said, 'It says "Archangel". It must be the ship's port of registration which means that it was a Russian ship.'

So the child who was saved from the sea was given the name of Archie Angel. He grew up to be a fine, strong man. In time he married and started a family, so there were Angels in Westray for around 150 years, before the name finally died out.

That is usually where the story ends, but my mother had a bit more of the story to add from her own family. My grandfather, Geordie Drever, was a schoolboy at the Skelwick School in Westray in the 1890s, when this story took place. He was in the same class as a boy called Henry Mason, whose mother was Mary Angel, the last person to bear that surname. My mother described her as, 'A coorse set buddy.'[51]

I always pictured her as looking like Boris Yeltsin in a headscarf and pinny.

At that time there was a head teacher at the Skelwick School who was a strict disciplinarian. No one got off with anything and if one pupil did something that annoyed him then the whole class were kept back to do extra work. It's called 'detention' these days, I believe. One day the whole class was kept behind for some misdemeanour and were scraping away on their slates, doing sums, when they could hear a 'mutter, mutter, mutter', coming up the kloss.[52] The door opened and in came Mary Angel, who said, 'Where's me boy?'

The teacher replied, 'He has been kept back as a punishment.'

'Well, his tea's ready,' replied Mary.

She went to get her son, but the teacher made an awful mistake, for anyone knows that it is a dangerous thing to get between a wild animal and their young. The teacher stepped in front of her, but she raised her fist and punched him and he fell to the floor in a heap. But this wasn't enough for Mary and she took the teacher by the scruff of the neck and beat his head on the ground until he was unconscious, then took her boy and went home.

The children were horrified.

'Mary Angel's killed the teacher! What kind of a detention will we get for that?'

They had visions of being old men with beards flowing to the ground, still sitting at their desks doing long division. Then one of the braver boys splashed some water on the teacher's face and his eyes flickered open.

'Get me a glass of water,' he said, in a faint voice.

The water was brought to him and he took a sip before saying, 'Class dismissed.'

They didn't need a second telling; they were out like a shot.

After that Mary Angel became a great hero among the children of the Skelwick School because from that day onward the teacher never again kept them behind in detention.

And so, dear reader, my book of tales has come to an end and I can say to you, 'Class dismissed!'

NOTES AND
EXPLANATIONS

1   Boy, you had better watch out that you don't catch the
    mother.
2   New Year's Eve.
3   Picts Houses.
4   Peedie means small in the Orkney dialect.
5   A cog is a drinking vessel made like half a barrel and is still
    used in Orkney weddings.
6   Pronounced Din-gis-how-ee.
7   Butter churn.
8   Moving house in attempted secrecy.
9   Karl Blind (1826–1907) was a German-born revolutionary,
    journalist and folklorist who took an interest in Shetland.
10 I am the queen of the sea, and Mermaid's my name,
    To show my fair body I do not think [a] shame,
    No clothes defile my skin, no dress will I wear,
    But the lovely bunches of my bonnie, bonnie hair.
11 Idiot.
12 Great Northern Diver.
13 Aurora Borealis, Northern Lights.
14 A small wooden stool.
15 Boat shelter cut into the shoreline

16   A shoe made of untanned hide, like a moccasin.

17   Cry.

18   Ask.

19   Witch.

20   A wooden chest where the 'meal' or flour was kept, packed tight to stop it from going mouldy.

21   A basket of woven straw worn on the back like a backpack, held in place by a band around the chest.

22   Kelp stems.

23   A mildly insulting term for a young woman.

24   Little.

25   A term of endearment, usually used on a child.

26   Screaming; screeching.

27   Chest.

28   It was a 'but and ben' house; the cooking and living area was the 'but' end and the bedroom was in the ben end.

29   Spring tide.

30   A geo is a ravine, a narrow cut into the coastline.

31   Reefs; submerged rocks.

32   The 'Clay Loan' in Kirkwall was the site of the gallows, on the high ground to the east of St Magnus Cathedral. In the seventeenth century the only house here on this road leading to the East Mainland was the Gallows Ha' (Hall), where the hangman lived, so the gallows (when built for an execution) would be clearly visible.

33   Strangled; garrotted with a piece of rope that was twisted tight by the hangman.

34   A small wooden vessel with one handle used to scoop water out of a bucket.

35   A term used to indicate a woman who had broken her oath of fidelity to a man.

36 A corruption of Vanderdecken, the captain of the phantom
    ship, the *Flying Dutchman*.

37 A number of Bronze Age barrows that lie near the shore.

38 A 'tusker' is an implement for cutting peats, while bister is a
    corruption of *bolstaðir*, the Old Norse word for a farm. So,
    'peat spade farm' could be the meaning of this name.

39 Farm or estate manager.

40 Free Church minister for Cross and Burness, Sanday, from
    1860–1903.

41 The term 'bitch' was commonly used in Orkney as an insult
    and could be applied to men, women, animals or inanimate
    objects. Strangely, the name for a female dog was a 'bikk', or
    'bikko' and was not associated with the word 'bitch'.

42 St Magnus.

43 Muckle = big. Whalp = a young dog; whelp.

44 A number of social-climbing Orcadians adopted a fake
    English accent to try and sound 'superior' – this was known
    locally as 'chanting' (speaking with English pronunciation).
    However, the veneer would often slip when they lost their
    temper, as is the case in this story.

45 A local law enforcer; a cross between a policeman, bailiff and
    sheriff officer.

46 'You can hold and I'll draw, until the cock of Grindley
    does crow.'

47 Get away with you, bare arse.

48 Chest.

49 Forespoken water was made by boiling water that contained
    stones from the shore, land and kirkyard while incantations
    are chanted over it.

50 Norwegian term for earl.

51 'A course set body', i.e. a large, overbearing person.

52 A passage between buildings.

BIBLIOGRAPHY

Almqvist, Bo, 'Some Orkney Traditions about Unbaptised Children',
  Béaloideas, the Journal of the Folklore of Ireland Society, Vol. 66
  (Dublin: The Folklore of Ireland Society, 1998).

Ben, Jo, *A Description of the Orchadian Islands* (1529), Margaret
  Hunter (trans., 1987).

Black, G.F., *County Folk-Lore Vol III, Orkney & Shetland Islands*
  (London: Folk-Lore Society, 1903).

Bremner, John, *Hoy, the Dark Enchanted Isle* (Kirkwall: Bellavista
  Publications, 1997).

Bruford, Alan (ed.), *The Green Man of Knowledge and other Scots
  Traditional Tales* (Aberdeen: Aberdeen University Press, 1982).

Bruford, A.J. and MacDonald, D.A. (ed.), *Scottish Traditional Tales*
  (Edinburgh: Polygon, 1994).

Crossley-Holland, Kevin, *Folk-Tales of the British Isles* (London:
  The Folio Society, 2007).

Dennison, Walter Traill, *The Orcadian Sketch Book* (Kirkwall:
  William Peace & Son, 1880).

Dennison, Walter Traill, *Orkney Folklore & Sea Legends* (Kirkwall:
  The Orkney Press Ltd, 1995).

Douglas, Sir George (ed.), *Scottish Fairy and Folk Tales* (London:
  Walter Scott Ltd, 1893).

Fergusson, R. Menzies, *Rambles in the Far North* (London: Alex Gardner, 1884).

Firth, Howie, *Tales of Long Ago* (Kirkwall: BBC Radio Orkney, 1986).

Gorrie, Daniel, *Summers and Winters in the Orkneys* (Kirkwall: William Peace).

Gunn, John (ed.), *The Orkney Book* (London: Thomas Nelson & Sons Ltd, 1906).

Mackintosh, W.R., *Around the Orkney Peat-Fires* (Kirkwall: The Orcadian, 1957).

Marwick, Ernest W., *An Anthology of Orkney Verse* (Kirkwall: W.R. Mackintosh, 1949).

Marwick, Ernest W., *The Folklore of Orkney and Shetland* (London: B.T. Batsford Ltd, 1975).

Marwick, Ernest W., *An Orkney Anthology Vol I* (Edinburgh: Scottish Academic Press, 1991).

Marwick, George, *George Marwick, the Collected Works of Yesnaby's Master Storyteller* (Kirkwall: The Orcadian Ltd, forthcoming).

Marwick, Hugh, 'Antiquarian Notes on Sanday', *Proceedings of the Orkney Antiquarian Society*, Vol. I, 1922–23, pp. 21–29 (Kirkwall: Orkney Antiquarian Society, 1923).

Marwick, Hugh, 'Antiquarian Notes on Rousay', *Proceedings of the Orkney Antiquarian Society*, Vol. II, 1923–24, pp. 15–21 (Kirkwall: Orkney Antiquarian Society, 1924).

Muir, Tom, *The Mermaid Bride and other Orkney Folk Tales* (Kirkwall: The Orcadian Ltd, 1998).

Muir, Tom, *The Storm Witch and other Westray Stories* (Westray: Westray Buildings Preservation Trust, 1999).

Muir, Tom, 'Tales and Legends', *The Orkney Book*, Omand, Donald (ed.), pp. 240–247 (Edinburgh: Birlinn Press, 2003).

Muir, Tom, *The Fiddler & The Trow* (Kirkwall: Orkney Islands Council).

Muir, Tom, *The Hogboon of Hellihowe* (Kirkwall: Orkney Islands Council).

Muir, Tom, *Assipattle and the Stoor Worm* (Kirkwall: Orkney Islands Council).

Muir, Tom, *The Shorter Orkneyinga Saga* (Kirkwall: Orkney Heritage, 2004).

Muir, Tom, *Orkney in the Sagas* (Kirkwall, Orkney Heritage, 2005).

Muir, Tom, 'Two Halloween Stories', *Snae*, Issue 1, pp. 90–94 (Papa Westray: Land Art Papa Westray, 2012).

Muir, Tom, 'Folktales of the Sea', *Snae*, Issue 2, pp. 160–167 (Papa Westray: Land Art Papa Westray, 2013).

Muir, Tom, *Tales from the Viking* Lands (Kirkwall: The Orcadian Ltd, forthcoming).

Mylne, Christine & Colin, *Glimpses of Eday Life Past and Present* (Kirkwall: The Orcadian Ltd, 1987).

Njal's Saga, Robert Cook (trans.) *The Complete Sagas of Icelanders* (Reykjavík: Leifur Eiríksson Publishing, 1997).

Rendall, Elsa, *Lest We Forget, a History of Westray* (Kirkwall: The Orcadian Ltd).

Robertson, Duncan J., 'Orkney Folk-Lore', *Proceedings of the Orkney Antiquarian Society*, Vol. II, 1922–23, pp. 29–37 (Kirkwall: Orkney Antiquarian Society, 1923).

Tatar, Maria (ed.), *The Annotated Classic Fairy Tales* (New York: W.W. Norton & Company, Inc., 2002).

Thomson, David, *The People of the Sea* (London: Turnstile Press, 1956).

Thomson, Gordon, *The Other Orkney Book* (Edinburgh: Northabout Publishing, 1980).

Towrie Cutt, Nancy and W., *The Hogboon of Hell and other Strange Orkney Tales* (London: Andre Deutsch, 1979).

Tudor, John R., *The Orkneys and Shetland, their past and present state* (London: Edward Stanford, 1883).

Uncredited, *Scottish Fairy Tales* (London: Bracken Books, 1993).

Wallace, Revd. James, *A Description of the Isles of Orkney, 1693* (Edinburgh: William Brown, 1883).

Wilson, Bryce, *Arthur Dearness & the Mermaid* (Kirkwall, Herald Publications, 2001).